Paving it ™
Forward

120 Pre-Paves That Will
Put You In The Passing Lane

ELISABETH FAYT

Paving It Forward™
120 Pre-Paves That Will
Put You In The Passing Lane

by ELISABETH FAYT
© 2009 ELISABETH FAYT. All rights reserved.

ISBN 978-1-60037-629-0 (hardcover)

ISBN 978-1-60037-628-3 (paperback)

Library of Congress Control Number 2009925283

Published by:

MORGAN · JAMES
THE ENTREPRENEURIAL PUBLISHER™
www.morganjamespublishing.com

Morgan James Publishing, LLC
1225 Franklin Ave. Ste 325
Garden City, NY 11530-1693
Toll Free 800-485-4943
www.MorganJamesPublishing.com

In an effort to support local communities, raise awareness and funds, Morgan James Publishing donates one percent of all book sales for the life of each book to Habitat for Humanity.
Get involved today, visit
www.HelpHabitatForHumanity.org.

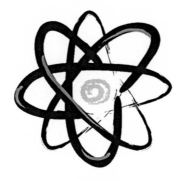

Dedicated to
Paramahansa Yogananda
in reverence.

And to my husband,
Anton Shouli,
for his everlasting friendship,
love and support.

TABLE OF CONTENTS

FOREWORD by Frank Maguire

The older I get, the more I realize the impact of visualization on life. I remember so well, when I was a young man, dreaming of things I wanted and realizing that eventually, if I stayed focused on them, those dreams would become reality! The questions I had to ask myself so often were, 'Was it a coincidence?' 'Was it the power of prayer?' or, 'Was it just a young boy dreaming his dreams?' As I grew older, I realized that the best way to create the future was to invent it! You are about to read a book that will show you how to create your future, one day at a time.

Elisabeth Fayt has created an instruction manual for you, showing you how to get what you want by "paving your life forward". Perhaps for the first time, you will learn how to make your dreams come true. We all have dreams. Many of us wonder why other people's dreams come true while we sit in a place of self-pity, not realizing that we have the same power as those who achieve their dreams.

How can your dreams come true if you don't have a dream?

Elisabeth shows you the way to connect your thoughts with your feelings and create the behavior that you are capable of. You wouldn't have a dream unless that dream was capable of becoming reality. It's inside of you! It always has been!

Think about your own life. How many times have you wondered how you were going to arrive at a certain place, a certain job, a certain position? You can do anything you dream of. It's wake up time; time for you to take charge of your life and this book shows you how to do just that!

Elisabeth is a spiritual teacher. She will teach you *the Law of Attraction* and the techniques of conscious intention that will line up your energy to create what you want. It's time for you to take over and control your life; to begin a journey that you have always longed for. This wonderful spiritual teacher will lead you on that journey.

I know that when you finish reading this book, your life will never be the same. I can tell you from my own personal experience that reading this book has made a great and significant change in my attitude. It has brought me peace, comfort, faith in myself, and has shed a bright light on my future. I'm a dreamer, just like you. We all are!

Enjoy your journey, my friend. You are not alone. There are many of us who, at this very moment, are on the journey with you.

Bon Voyage

Frank Maguire
CEO and Founder – The Maguire Group*
Founding Senior Executive – Fed Ex
www.frankmaguire.com

* AN INTERNATIONAL GROUP OF RESOURCES CREATING CORPORATE CULTURE AND PERSONAL COMMUNICATIONS PROGRAMS.

ACKNOWLEDGEMENTS

I sincerely acknowledge the following individuals for their impact on my life and the creation of this book...

... with reverence, Paramahansa Yogananda, my spiritual teacher since 1993. Paramahansa Yogananda is a great Indian Saint, whose message has made a massive shift in the Earth's consciousness in the last century. He is most renowned for authoring the spiritual classic, *Autobiography of a Yogi*. I urge you to pick up a copy if you are interested in metaphysics or Eastern philosophy. *Paving It Forward* is speckled with nuggets of wisdom from Yogananda's teachings. It is because of this great Saint that I have the knowledge and inspiration to share my message with you.

... with deepest affection, my husband Anton Shouli. Anton is responsible for the title of this book, as well as hour-upon-hour of editorial assistance. He could very easily be considered an unofficial co-author of *Paving It Forward*. I thank him for his support and belief in me, always. As I commit to inspiring others, he continues to inspire me. I adore him, my mentor, my soulmate, my best friend.

... my Reiki Master/teacher, Elizabeth Gilberg. Elizabeth introduced me to the Energy behind the Law of Attraction through her intensive study program offered only to Reiki Masters. It became clear to me early on that my life was not the only one about to change. I discovered my gift was to teach all people, not just trained healers, about Pre-Paving.

... Anna-Mae Sebastian and Angela Hook for their hours, days and weeks of editorial and design.

... Rick Frishman and the team at Morgan James Publishing for their professional guidance and for believing in my message.

... Dr. John Demartini, Marci Shimoff and Ron Joyce for endorsing this project amidst their busy schedules.

... Frank Maguire for writing the Foreword to this book and for being the beautiful Soul he is, an honor to call "friend".

I feel very lucky to have drawn such talented people to me throughout the process of publishing this book. The Universe, without fail, sends us those people we need to carry out our worthwhile goals. *Paving It Forward* has been made possible by the collaborated efforts of special people, for whom I am sincerely grateful.

INTRODUCTION

M ost simply put, the purpose of this book is to shift your way of thinking, to expand your consciousness, so you can create the life you desire.

Everything you think about, you attract, so your thoughts have a tremendous impact on life as you experience it. Without a proven technique for staying positive, it can be easy to slip into a negative state of mind without realizing it. Even if you are generally positive by nature, life will throw curve balls. You need to be prepared. *Paving it Forward* will teach you just that, how to be prepared by pre-paving your future.

Pre-paving is a method of conscious creation. It is similar to the practice of affirmation but different in that it does not require repetition. A pre-pave is a statement of action or belief that you put forward to the Universe as a command. You mold your life by telling the Universe what you want. In this book you will learn about the energy of thought so that you understand how your thoughts create. Without this important understanding of **how**, there can be little motivation to change. When the understanding hits you between the eyes, you will want to begin consciously pre-paving right away.

THE LAW OF ATTRACTION

Things of the same vibration or frequency are attracted to one another. Like attracts like.

I f you are a big fan of the Law of Attraction, but have spent any time at all doubting its power, pre-paving will change your doubt to belief. It is the tool that will make you a true believer. It changes the consciousness from a re-active state to a pro-active one.

This book will teach you the basics of pre-paving, and give you many examples of pre-paves you can use right away in every avenue of life. Personal stories and examples help you to truly understand how the energy works in different life scenarios and how you can manipulate the energy for the result you desire. Once you catch on to the technique of pre-paving, you will see how easy it is to stay positive at all times. You will be able to shift your consciousness on a dime, whenever you notice the need to change your thought.

Each chapter focuses on a different aspect of life. If you feel inclined, use the table of contents and go directly to the area of life that you wish to enhance. Or choose to start from the beginning and work your way through in succession to the end. Mixed in with the pre-paves is counsel in all areas, from addictions to changing habits, to finding peace and balance. Nuggets of wisdom are hidden in the stories and analogies. Be sure to read all of the chapters, whether you think they apply to you or not. For example, if you are not currently working, it is still important to read *Paving It Forward - at Work* because that chapter carries within it a wealth of wisdom on how to be successful in life in general, not just at the office. Some chapters have several pre-paves and others have only a few poignant ones that will help you. There are an endless number of pre-paves you can create for yourself on any topic. It is truly limitless. Practice *paving it forward* with the examples in this book. Then as you get good at pre-paving you will find yourself creating your own pre-paves all day that are unique to you and what you are going through at that specific moment.

Repetition is a big part of the learning process when you are shifting your consciousness to positive habits of thought. There are some important concepts repeated in different sections with unique analogies to drive home the point. Certain habits of negative thought may have worked against you in the past. You need to lift the needle of your attention and shift it to a new spot, dropping it down onto a place that is in line with manifesting what you want. At first the spot is slippery until it becomes a habit. This takes repetition. Some of the key points as they emerge in different situations are important to review several times in order to clearly get the full meaning of the concept. Each concept, when discussed in a different frame of life brings on its own learning and power that will help you apply it in your daily life regardless of the context. It really is quite simple. Repetition of a few key concepts is integral to learning.

I welcome you to practice this new way of thinking. It means to pre-pave your life before and as it happens, rather than reacting as a victim to what you feel life might have arbitrarily dished out. Make pre-paving your own and allow the new energy you project change your life.

People spend more time choosing what they are going to wear in the morning than they do choosing how they will connect with people, how they will feel, or what they will accomplish.

Pre-paving is consciously choosing how you want to look, live and feel through every part of your day and every part of your life. You might say, "If only life were so simple." I say, "Yes, it is", and I will prove it to you.

Pre-paving is telling the Universe what you want before it happens. It is a form of intention that "lines up the energy" so that you can easily manifest what you desire. Whether you realize it or not, all day you are intending, and what you intend you create. You create with your thoughts. In essence, you are already pre-paving, although sometimes you have been pre-paving positively and other times negatively. What you have attracted is the result of what you have consciously or unconsciously paved forward. In other words, whatever you are pre-paving, you are creating. Suddenly the idea of pre-paving catches your attention.

> *People spend more time choosing what they are going to wear in the morning than they do choosing how they will connect with people, how they will feel, or what they will accomplish.*

Pre-paving is about setting your intention. I am a Reiki Master*, so I like to explain things in terms of energy. When you know the energy behind what thoughts do to your life, you get very motivated to make a change for the positive. Imagine that you have a field of energy immediately surrounding your body, about six inches around your body if you are picturing it. Every thought you think enters this energy field. This energy field is called your vibration. It is the sum of the thoughts, feelings and intentions that you are currently holding.

Your vibration works as a magnet, attracting to you all of the people, events and circumstances in your life.

*Reiki is an ancient Japanese form of hands-on healing. A Reiki practitioner must pass through certain levels of training before being called a Master and with this title is also qualified to teach it and bestow it upon others.

Your goal is to raise your vibration so you begin attracting the good things in life that you have always wanted. The moment you begin positively pre-paving, your vibration rises immediately.

HOW IT WORKS

Every thought you think is recorded in the ether and starts to manifest. It manifests according to the degree of energy, conviction and power you give it. When you pre-pave with conviction and belief, you make significant changes in your life in a short period of time. In other words, you change your destiny.

A pre-pave is a statement that tells the Universe what you will do, how you will feel, or what will happen. It is a statement that you can either say verbally (loudly or softly), or you can write it down, or think it mentally. Whichever way feels right for you is fine, but know this; the more power you put into your pre-pave, the more powerful the result.

Think of a hypnotist in action. A hypnotist puts the conscious mind to sleep and within thirty seconds can have you thinking you are a red fire engine. We hypnotize ourselves every moment of the day with the thoughts we choose to hold and the words we choose to speak. The sub-conscious mind cannot distinguish between reality and a wish. It also cannot take a joke. When you think or say something, the sub-conscious mind says "Okay, let's support this because it must be true". Even when you are joking around, saying things in jest, you are creating what you are saying.

The Universe can't take a joke. When you think or say something, the sub-conscious mind says "Okay, let's support this because it must be true".

The sub-conscious mind carries within itself your entire belief system. It works on automatic pilot. It never stops, even when you are sleeping. It creates what has been programmed into it by your conscious mind. If you say things like "I can't afford it" or "That's the story of my life", the sub-conscious mind takes this as reality and orchestrates everything around you to make it come true. If you are joking around with your spouse and you say something to the effect of "I do everything around here", the Universe will manifest more and more situations where you are doing more than your share around the house.

This is where pre-paving comes in. Pre-paving is a conscious, positive programming of the sub-conscious mind. When you place a positive command into your sub-conscious mind, it starts working immediately toward making it happen. This is the power of your thought and spoken word. This is the power of pre-paving. Positive pre-paving is consciously choosing your thoughts and words for a specific result. When you set a pre-pave in motion, it physically "lines up the energy" for its manifestation.

When you pre-pave, you are never in the wrong place at the wrong time, because the Universe "lines up the energy" for you to be in the right place at the right time.

What does it mean to "line up the energy"? Let's look at the analogy of your daily commute to work. If you get in the car and pre-pave safety, the Universe will physically orchestrate circumstances around you in order to keep you safe. On the other hand, if you do not pre-pave safety as you start your car, you personally may not have accident-consciousness, but the driver next to you may. The result is that you could wind up in an accident situation just for being in the wrong place at the wrong time. How many times have you found yourself there, "the wrong place at the wrong time"? This is not by chance. These things can be avoided by positive pre-paving. When you pre-pave, you are never in the wrong place at the wrong time, because the Universe "lines up the energy" for you to be in the right place at the right time.

You do not need extra time in the day to pre-pave. You are already doing it. It is a matter of practicing it consciously, practicing it positively and choosing pre-paves to create specifically what you want.

The most powerful times to pre-pave are first thing in the morning and last thing at night. These are the times that your consciousness is most powerful for creating. It is when the consciousness is changing from the wakeful state to the sub-conscious state and back again. Unfortunately, this tends to be the time that most people worry. Worry is a negative pre-pave. Worrying at this time of night and morning is the worst negative pre-pave of all. The comforting thing to know is that a positive thought is one hundred times more powerful than a negative one. Don't beat yourself up if you have a fleeting negative thought. The next time you have a negative thought, immediately turn it into the opposite, positive pre-pave. Know that in an instant, you can wipe out the negative thought, one hundred fold. Imagine your life if you could turn all of your worries into positive pre-paves.

There are times when you will want to pre-pave a specific outcome that you desire because you have so clearly etched into your mind what you want. In this case, the more clearly you picture it and know what you want, the better. There will be other times, however, when you will want to pave forward an outcome that is open-ended, not to limit yourself. I have found my greatest achievement to be when I have left the results open, shooting for the stars and reaching the moon. You will understand more as you read on and begin to practice for yourself.

Pave it forward with conviction. Feel it and mean it. Your pre-pave will be as powerful as your passion and belief. My life has been dramatically changed with pre-paving which is why I have made it the focus of my teaching. I have personally recovered from addictions, moods and a string of self-sabotaging tendencies. My life went from mediocre to phenomenal with this amazing technique of conscious creation. In my classes, I have witnessed what it does for people. Pre-paving makes a shift in your consciousness, so much that if you could see energy, you would physically see your vibration change as you instigate each positive command.

MAKING IT A HABIT

When you understand the principles of pre-paving, with a little practice, you can literally pave forward every segment of your day to receive the outcome of your choice. This is your ultimate goal. It brings you into a state of constant awareness. When you can spend your entire day in a state of conscious creation, then you can truly say you are awake. Otherwise, you are spending part of your life sleep-walking with your internal switch on auto-pilot, creating by default.

A good place to start is to take things one day at a time. That is why pre-paves are most successful, especially in the beginning, when you include **today** in your promise. The goal is not to practice just one day, but to practice and experience your power with baby steps. Give it your all, and watch things change around you according to your changed thought. It is much easier to promise to live according to a certain plan for one full day than it is to commit to a lifetime of perfection. However, the goal is to turn the positive pre-pave into habit. This comes with daily practice in **today** mode. If you do enough **today** pre-paves, eventually, sooner than you think, you will be able to accomplish your goals as life-long habits. You must believe what you pave forward in order for it to work. To believe it, you make it simple by making changes one day at a time. By practicing it daily over a period of time, you will be able to confidently believe that you can continue its practice over the course of your life.

I say this most sincerely; if you can even take one pre-pave and practice it wholeheartedly once, you have made a shift in the right direction! The mind is a tricky thing. When you are paving it forward, you are in control. You are the magician in charge of the trick. If you are not conscious of what you are paving forward with your thoughts, then you are creating by default and the trick is on you.

To begin the process of making pre-paving a habit, ask yourself these two questions several times throughout the day: "How do I feel?" and "What do I want?" These two questions are the most important to tune into and consciously create, because if you are going to create something, you need to know what you want. If you want a dream to come true, you need to have a dream.

Use your emotional guidance system to tell you when you need to pre-pave. Negative feelings are a blessing, a gift. They tell you when your thoughts are not on track. When you feel a negative feeling, it is a sign that your thoughts are not taking you in the direction you want to go. When you ask yourself throughout the day, "How do I feel?" and you discover you are feeling a negative emotion, you have the opportunity to change your thought immediately before it has a chance to manifest! You then ask yourself "What do I want?" and change your thought by putting a positive pre-pave into your consciousness to receive the result you seek and you do this according to what it is that you want. "How do I feel and what do I want?" In other words, "I'm feeling this way, how can I feel good again?"

There is nothing more important in the Law of Attraction than feeling good, because what you are feeling, you are manifesting.

There is nothing more important in the Law of Attraction than feeling good, because what you are feeling, you are manifesting. Asking yourself what you want will tell you what you need to pre-pave. Always listen to the first thing that your mind brings forward. This is your Intuition speaking to you. If you do not know what you want, then practice any pre-pave that will take you to the positive. Then intend that you will discover what it is that you want at a later time. Methods of strengthening your Intuition are discussed in a later chapter.

To recap, once you have identified a negative feeling, this is the perfect time to pre-pave. Send a command of what you want out into the Universe. For example, if you discover you are feeling lonely because you don't have a life partner, then pre-pave with conviction that you will find the mate of your dreams. Believe that this person is being drawn to you right now with the power of your command. Visualize what this person might look like. Feel how happy you would feel enjoying his or her company.

The alternative is to remain in the negative state. Wallowing in negativity pushes away the very thing you desire. This is the most important time to pre-pave! Do you see the blessing in being aware of your feelings, acknowledging them and pivoting them to the positive by pre-paving? Feelings are marvelous. Allow them to guide you.

> *Feelings are not a result of your circumstances; feelings are a result of your state of mind.*

Your feelings have the greatest power to create, more than anything else, but you must realize where feelings originate. It is a common misconception that feelings are a result of circumstance. On the contrary, your feelings are a result of your state of mind; a result of the thoughts you choose to think. When you think a certain way, you will feel a certain way. Your thoughts are by choice not by chance. In essence, your feelings are something you choose, they do not happen because of your surrounding environment.

Continuing with the same example, if you choose to think about how you haven't met your soul mate yet, projecting that you will be spending the next holiday alone again, you will create feelings of loneliness. Instead, focus on being the best you can be so that you attract a wonderful person. Pre-pave that this person is being drawn to you and you will begin to feel happy. You put yourself into alignment to receive your mate. This is why pre-paving is such a powerful technique of creating consciously. You choose your thoughts by pre-paving. You choose your feelings by your thoughts. Practice and memorize the pre-paves in this book that resonate with you the most. In your times of greatest emotional need, they will be there in your consciousness, ready to "line up the energy" for success.

W hat do you do when you have pre-paved something, but the Universe seemingly sends you something different? This is the time to hold on to your conviction. Be sure first that what you are intending is what you truly want, then hold tightly to your desire. Sometimes past bad karma* or the result of past negative thoughts will bring into your current experience something that appears to go against what you want. If you acknowledge it as a manifestation of past thought and keep focused on your current positive pre-pave with sustained effort, you **will** create what you want. I have heard it said in this way: what you have in your life right now is not who you are, it's who you were. Who you are right now is what you are thinking about right now.

Often people give up too soon, surrendering to a plan gone wrong because they lose faith. They lower their vibration with their frustration or disappointment. When you pre-pave what you want, no plan can go wrong, it is Law. Pre-pave what you want and sustain your thought on the positive, despite any evidence to the contrary. It will, and must, manifest. The moment you launch a desire, it is already being created. But when you doubt or question how it will materialize, you send a message to the Universe that cancels out your creation. Doubt is a negative pre-pave. Remember this.

To help see your creation through, after pre-paving what you want, make it a habit to hold onto a thought of gratitude that it is already done. When you pre-pave with gratitude, it is sure to manifest.

Another way to keep your thought on a high plane, especially if you feel doubt creeping in, is to take your mind off what you are creating momentarily. Focus your mind on anything that will raise your vibration. An example is to think of someone or something that makes you happy. Filling your energy field with positive thoughts will raise your vibration and you will be given many signs that the Law of Attraction is positively working in your life. As humans, sometimes we need proof to truly believe something with conviction. Raise your vibration and you will receive all of the proof you need to show you that you are the creator of your life.

---

* KARMA: THE LAW OF CAUSE AND EFFECT, WHAT YOU SOW YOU WILL REAP.

The first step is awareness. You are affirming all of the time, either in word, speech or action. Become aware of what you are projecting. Change your inner and outer dialogue to that of a positive pre-pave where you are in control of your destiny. The goal of pre-paving is to consciously create. When you put positive thoughts into your energy field, you raise your vibration. Your vibration is your magnet.

Study the pre-paves on the following pages. Connect with those that resonate within you the most. Commit to practicing them regularly. Create your own. Tune into your emotional guidance system and make pre-paving not only a daily, but a moment-to-moment habit. Even just a few words, positively pre-paved, will put you in a different state of consciousness immediately. It can change everything.

Pre-pave with conviction and a feeling of gratitude. In changing your thoughts, you change what you resonate out into the Universe and, hence, what the Universe brings back to you.

PAVING IT FORWARD
in the Morning

PAVING IT FORWARD – IN THE MORNING

As mentioned, morning is one of the most important times to pre-pave. As your consciousness shifts from the sleep state to wakefulness, your thoughts at this time are the most powerful. Unfortunately, it is the time most people spend in worry. They worry about the day ahead or feel anxious about all that has to be accomplished. Worry and anxiety are negative pre-paves.

Every thought you think either empowers or dis-empowers you. Your first morning thoughts are critical in setting the tone for the day. When you are truly aware of this, you can be a powerful creator by making your very first thought a Masterpiece. What Masterpiece do you want to create today? Pre-pave it.

PRE-PAVE in the Morning

I feel great today.

PRE-PAVE: *I feel great today.*

This pre-pave can change your health, your attitude and of course, what you attract. Your feelings have the greatest power to attract because it is your feelings that strongly resonate vibrations out into the world. You receive according to the frequency of feeling that you emit. In other words, how you feel will determine the nature of the life you create for yourself. No matter what happens in the day, if you feel great, you will manifest good things. What a motivation to use this pre-pave.

I am rarely sick. I don't even get the common cold. Every day I pre-pave that I will feel great, and I do. It doesn't mean that life's challenges go away, but it does have a great effect on how I deal with them. This pre-pave brings good health and a mental state of happiness.

You can decide how you are going to feel before the day starts. A pre-pave is a command you give the Universe of what you want. Tell the Universe how you want to feel today and every day.

PRE-PAVE in the Morning

Something wonderful
is going to happen today.

PRE-PAVE: *Something wonderful is going to happen today.*

I love this pre-pave because, like others, it works. Something wonderful always does happen. Say it with conviction, and gratitude, knowing that it will manifest.

Wonderful things are happening all around you all of the time. When you intend them, the Universe opens your eyes to them. In essence, the energy of your intention wakes you up to see what is already there.

Imagine the missed opportunities and wonderful experiences lost when you are on auto-pilot. Wake up and see what the Universe has in store for you today. With this pre-pave you are telling the Universe, "Surprise me!"

PRE-PAVE in the Morning

Today I will deeply connect
with people.

PRE-PAVE: *Today I will deeply connect with people.*

How you connect with people is a choice. If you decide in the morning that you will connect deeply with others, then you will. It is as simple as that.

Carry this pre-pave with you throughout the day. Each time you come in contact with someone, pre-pave that you will speak and listen on a high level of truth. That means to communicate with sincerity, integrity and non-judgment. Your intentions are very powerful. If you are not consciously intending, you are creating by default. Enter the energy mix of others into the equation and you may get a result for which you hadn't quite bargained.

Take care of your own energy first by putting intentions of truth and sincerity into all of your exchanges.

PRE-PAVE in the Morning

Today, I easily accomplish
all I need to.

PRE-PAVE: *Today, I easily accomplish all I need to.*

One of the most common complaints I hear from people is lack of time. They say they don't have time to exercise, read or do the things they love. This is a negative pre-pave. It sets you up for failure. If you truly want or love something badly enough, you will make the time to do it. You have as much time as your intention allows.

Time is not found. It is made.

Change your thought to one that pre-paves plenty of time to get everything done, easily and effortlessly. You choose what you accomplish before the day starts. Often, you can get something done in the time it takes to complain about not having enough time to do it. When you pre-pave enough time, you will also find balance and peace of mind.

There is a profound quote I used in the media launch of my spa, RnR Wellness, when our doors opened in December of 2004. This quote still hangs on my wall at the reception desk and adorns the center page of my spa brochure. "Time is not found. It is made." If you knew my life and what I accomplish in a day, you would know that I live by this.

PRE-PAVE in the Morning

Today I make a fresh start.

PRE-PAVE: *Today I make a fresh start.*

Where you put your attention, there is your energy for creating. The past only belongs to you if you bring it into your vibration today. This is a very important point. Read it slowly. Your past has no part of you any longer, unless you bring it into your vibration right now, by giving it your attention.

Where you put your attention, there is your energy for creating.

One of my favorite stories to tell is about two monks walking alongside a river in the Himalayan Mountains. They were approached by a woman in tears who begged them to help her cross the river. The rapids were so strong that, alone, she would not have been assured a safe journey to the other side. The senior monk agreed immediately to carry her across, at which time the other monk spoke up very seriously. "You can't do this, Brother. You know our vows. We aren't allowed to touch a woman let alone carry her. What are you thinking?" But the senior monk silenced him and continued to help the woman across the river. After carrying her safely to the other side, the two monks continued their journey toward their destination back to the monastery. All the while, the young monk kept repeating his astonishment that the senior monk had breached his vows. He repeated his concern for almost half an hour until finally the senior monk calmly responded, "Yes, I picked up the woman. Yes, I carried her across the river. There I set her down. You are still carrying her."

If you focus on what you've left behind, you will never be able to see what lies ahead.

When you pre-pave a fresh start, you consciously release the past. Keep the lesson. Release the rest. Each day is an opportunity to make a fresh start.

PRE-PAVE in the Morning

I expect the best.

PRE-PAVE: *I expect the best.*

Extensive psychological studies have been conducted in the United States with classrooms of junior high school students. In one specific experiment, one teacher was assigned a class whom she was told was full of over-achievers, highly intelligent students with the potential of becoming great leaders. Another teacher was assigned a class whom she was told was full of academically and socially problematic students. In reality, however, whatever they were told, they were given the opposite.

By the end of the semester, the students were rated by the teachers at their final exams. One teacher flunked the entire class, noting the students to be unmanageable and "not suitable for entry into the next grade". These were actually the highly intelligent students who had been the previous year noted as exceptional in their class. This teacher's expectations of a problematic class completely shaped what she saw and experienced of her students. Not surprisingly, the opposite transpired with the other test class.

What do you expect in your life? What do you expect from your spouse, your family members, your colleagues? Your expectations become your intentions. Often expectations are so deeply rooted in the sub-conscious mind that you don't realize they are there. If you've expected things to happen a certain way for so long, you have been unconsciously creating them all along. Today, become aware of your expectations and start to shift your expectations to the outcome that you want.

PRE-PAVE in the Morning

Today is a gift.

PRE-PAVE: *Today is a gift.*

I had the privilege of meeting Carmel Maguire recently. Carmel is the wife of Frank Maguire*, co-founder of Fed-Ex. From the moment I sat down to dinner with Carmel, I knew this woman was special. In the first few moments of meeting, she invited my family to their home in California for dinner. She had us in stitches the whole evening with her stories and life experiences. At 71 years of age, this feisty lady shared with us that, "When you reach seventy, you become bullet-proof". She said, "Today's seventies are like what our fifties used to be years ago", and this is so true. People age like wine, we get better.

The thing she said that impacted me the most was that, "At seventy, every day you wake up alive is a gift". This should be at any age. Life is a gift. Although I had heard this a thousand times, and also teach it, I heard this woman say the words and felt as though I was hearing them for the first time. Sometimes, it takes the right person to say the same words in the right way for it to sink in.

Life is a gift. If you start each day with this thought, and carry it through your day, your life will make a drastic change for the better.

PRE-PAVE in the Morning

It's going to be a great day.

PRE-PAVE: *It's going to be a great day.*

My young nephew, Neil, is a true example of a positive thinker. His parents have instilled this way of thinking into him since birth. It is also part of his natural character. He is one of those incredible kids you love to have around because he emanates positive energy all of the time. On his first day of grade one, Neil was asked how his day went. Neil answered with a straight face, "Not good". He paused for a moment, then a grin broke out on his face and he continued with a passionate voice, "It was great!"

Face it; you've had good days and bad. These alternating good and bad days happen when you're not consciously paving your thoughts. Instead, you're creating by default. Why not create only good days? You can do this by pre-paving that your day will not only be good, but great! The type of day you have is totally dependent on your thoughts. It has very little to do with your circumstances. When you know this, then you will put the power of your whole being into this morning pre-pave and you will tell the Universe that your day will be great. This pre-pave is one of my personal favorites.

My husband, Anton, recently built our home, at perhaps one of the worst times to build in Calgary, where we live. The economy was booming and there was an over-abundance of construction taking place. Finding contractors was the first challenge. Getting them to show up was the next. It wasn't a bed of roses for Anton. I could see his frustration at times, but I must say he was so good at using the Law of Attraction that he would rarely express any frustration at all despite the magnitude of challenges I was sure he was facing daily. There were days that I could sense things were heating up on the job site. It was on those mornings that I would poke my head into the washroom as he was shaving and I would remind him with passion, "Remember, it's going to be a great day today!" I would always get a smile. A smile already shifts your energy in the right direction! I can tell you for certain that when we would re-convene that night, he would, in fact, share that all things did go his way that day. That's the power of paving it forward!

PRE-PAVE in the Morning

I love my life.

PRE-PAVE: *I love my life.*

If you want a passionate life, practice this pre-pave and mean it. It is a great way to get yourself into a state of gratitude first thing in the morning. When you love your life, the Universe gives you more reasons to love your life. Life has its challenges and it has its easy roads, but if you look at it all equally with love and passion, it becomes beautiful, and you attract to yourself more experiences of beauty.

> Being passionate about life is not about magically living in an environment that you believe meets your requirements for happiness. Being passionate about life is choosing to love it. Paving your day forward with love and appreciation will create a life of passion.

The environment you are in right now is perfect for you. It is a complete recipe of what your Soul needs right at this very moment in time to progress, especially the tests. All circumstances have a purpose and a lesson. Love it all. Think of your life as a great novel. A great novel has an exciting plot with twists and turns. Each chapter unfolds a new understanding of the characters and where everything is going. How amazing our lives are, and how they intertwine with the lives of others.

Spend time every morning in a state of gratitude for the incredible life you have. Being passionate about life is not about magically living in an environment that you believe meets your requirements for happiness. Being passionate about life is choosing to love it. Paving your day forward with love and appreciation will create a life of passion.

PAVING IT FORWARD
at Work

I maintained a position for ten years that some people would have deemed glamorous. In reality, not many could have persevered. I was the Executive Assistant to one of Canada's most prominent entrepreneur-billionaires, Ron Joyce, co-founder of Tim Hortons*. I joined Mr. Joyce in 1995 just around the time that he sold his company to Wendy's* International. Without a doubt, his life was exciting and very much in the public eye. A few years later, at the age of 65, he liquified his holdings and decided to play with his fortune. I was pulled from the day-to-day operation to assist him as he built his personal dreams. One dream of his was to build a premier 27-hole golf course on the shores of Nova Scotia. Today *Fox Harb'r* stands as one of Canada's top-rated golf courses where the likes of Bobby Orr, Tiger Woods and President Clinton have played. Another dream of Mr. Joyce's was to launch a super-yacht during America's Cup in New Zealand. His yacht, Destination *Fox Harb'r*, did indeed launch during the Cup festivities; then made its journey around the world.

> Your work environment is a reflection of your state of mind.

As Mr. Joyce's assistant, I traveled the globe. I lived in his homes and basically dedicated my life to serving him. Not many could have handled the demands of such a position. For me, it was a training ground. For several years prior, I had been a sincere student of the healing arts and the Law of Attraction as taught by the Masters of India, primarily Paramahansa Yogananda. Immersed in this new all-encompassing lifestyle geared toward service, I was able to put the teachings to the test. I was blessed so often with opportunities to study with spiritual Masters around the world during my business travels. I took any opportunity I could to learn, including spending my vacation time in intensive study. I sincerely practiced the principles in my job and I made it my business to find peace in its least expected place, the busy corporate world.

---

*Tim Hortons is a Canadian donut and coffee chain Ron Joyce co-founded with hockey great Tim Horton. Today, the chain is a house-hold name in Canada.

*Wendy's is an international hamburger chain founded by Dave Thomas. Many of the Wendy's stores have Tim Hortons stores right next to them under one roof. These combination stores are called Tim/Wen Combos.

I used the teachings right from the beginning. I remember the first few years when I had just joined Tim Hortons. I reported to both Ron Joyce as well as Jim Rushak, the vice-president of Western Canada. In the beginning, I worked more closely with Jim than Ron. Jim was a phenomenal leader, but in the beginning, provided me with some of my most difficult tests of all. I was warned by colleagues when I joined the company that three Executive Assistants had preceded me in the previous year. I understood in a very short time why. The environment was challenging. No matter what I did, Jim's mannerisms spoke loudly and clearly to me that he seemed displeased with my performance. I don't mind telling you, I was an exceptional business-woman, a previous restaurant-owner, a university graduate with business awards and a sincere passion for the Executive Assistant profession, not to mention a typing speed of over a hundred words per minute. I was giving it my all. What more could I do? To quit would have been to admit defeat. That wasn't my style. I told myself that I would continue to give it my all. Despite his attitude toward me, I pledged to keep my own vibration high. I focused on positive thoughts and on pre-paving a positive outcome each day. I kept asking the Universe to "show me how to serve this man", and I focused on serving him. I resonated "service". I went above and beyond. I persevered.

Within a few weeks, a magical change happened within Jim. His whole demeanor was different. He became very open and friendly. He started to show great appreciation for everything I did for him. He began to rely on me. He allowed me to take over major projects and areas of the business. He put his trust in my skills and initiative. He started to focus on how he could serve me. Could he get me a coffee? Was I happy? How could he make the environment better for me? This complete and utter transformation happened within a three-week period of me holding my vibration high and pre-paving a positive outcome. The following several years were an amazing journey of learning and accomplishment working with these two great leaders. I attribute my success to maintaining a high vibration of thought at all times. I was given the most amazing gift of putting the law of attraction and pre-paving to the test. It worked like a charm, every time, without fail.

My years with Tim Hortons were, as I said, a great training-ground. Everything in life is. It prepares you for the next phase, especially the challenges. It gives you the experience you need and builds character for withstanding your next set of opportunities. In my case, my experiences with Tim Hortons prepared me to build my own dream, RnR Wellness. My vision was to open an exquisite spa within a beautiful hotel. I approached all of the four-star hotel chains in Calgary looking for space, but kept coming up with the same response, that there was "no room at the inn". Most of the hotel managers were sincerely trying to carve out some space for me. It was in their best interest to provide a spa offering to their guests. At the end of the day, it just wasn't going to happen. I, on the other hand, wasn't going to take "No" for an answer.

Instead of wallowing in discouragement, I took this opportunity to pre-pave open-ended success. I had no idea what that would look like or where it would lead, but I knew there was an opportunity around the corner much greater and grander than I could imagine. Then came the brilliant idea.

I contacted David Connor, the general manager at the Westin Hotel and proposed this; "What if I provided you with an entire spa menu, right in the comfort of the guest room, and you didn't have to give me any space at all?" He was thrilled. He put me in front of his board and I pitched the idea showing a gorgeous mock up of an 'in-room spa menu'.

The decision was unanimous. The idea was accepted with cheers and embraces. I felt like I had all of a sudden enlarged my family. This was the result of choosing to pre-pave success rather than accepting defeat.

Over the next several months, I pre-paved that I would launch one new hotel satellite spa each month and I did just that. I opened spas in the Sheraton, Delta and Marriott chains all within the following three months. It was around that time that I found a physical space for my main spa. It was the perfect spot right along the Bow River. It was close to the hotels, but in a serene spot that would be perfect for the experience I was creating.

Today, RnR Wellness has a satellite spa in all of Calgary's major hotels with plans underway for expansion into US and international markets. In this book, I speak to you as an Executive Assistant, as a student of the great spiritual Masters of India, as a spa owner and entrepreneur and, lastly, as an international author/speaker on the Law of Attraction. My intent is to prove to you that you can pave forward the life you want. Without a shadow of a doubt, the last two decades of my work life are proof of the power of pre-paving. The work you do is an expression of who you are. Your work environment is a creation of your thought.

PRE-PAVE at Work

I arrive early for work and
mentally prepare for the day.

PRE-PAVE: *I arrive early for work and mentally prepare for the day.*

The day goes 100% better when you start it ahead of the eight ball instead of behind it. When you take the time to arrive a little early, the mental state that follows is one of calmness. You have time to grab your coffee, look at your to-do list and pre-pave some priorities of what you want to accomplish.

On the other hand, when you arrive just a little late, perhaps you arrive as your phone is on its sixth ring. You receive a dirty look from a colleague who has already been there thirty minutes. Already you get the feeling of being overwhelmed. If you put thoughts of "being overwhelmed" into your vibration, the Universe will bring you more scenarios throughout the day to overwhelm you. That is how the energy of the Law of Attraction works.

Just by arriving a little early to mentally prepare, your whole day changes, because the energy and thought you put into your vibration is different. It makes you feel good inside, and it creates an environment that helps you to enjoy your job. When you enjoy what you do, you will **want** to arrive in time to prepare to have an awesome day.

> *The more I want to get something done,*
> *the less I call it work.*
>
> *– Richard Bach*

PRE-PAVE at Work

I am valued for what I do.

PRE-PAVE: *I am valued for what I do.*

My first few years working for Ron Joyce had me stationed in the Tim Horton's Calgary office, working in a corporate office environment. Up until that point, I had been in the entrepreneurial world, co-owning a small chain of restaurants in southern Alberta, so the corporate structure was a bit of an adjustment. I didn't seem to fit in with the norm of the office chatter and water cooler talk. I used to notice that the people who complained they weren't getting raises were those who loved to talk about their value rather than provide it.

If you want to be valued in your job, give value to your boss and the company. It's that simple. When you focus on giving value rather than talking about how you are under-paid or under-appreciated, you attract the acknowledgement, the position and the raise.

If you think that your work situation will not be affected by negative thinking, think again. Every thought you think regarding your job sits in your energy field and immediately starts to manifest itself, whether your boss is listening or not. That is the important thing to remember. It is not about you and your boss. It is about you and the Universe, the Source of all abundance. The raise does not come from your boss, it comes from the Source. It comes when you begin to vibrate your true worth. The Universe is always watching and listening, to your thoughts, words and actions. You are rewarded according to what you are vibrating.

Whoever does not love his work,
cannot hope that it will please others.

– Unknown

PRE-PAVE at Work

I work with enthusiasm today.

PRE-PAVE: *I work with enthusiasm today.*

Enthusiasm generates willpower. If you want to increase your sales and work more efficiently with less errors, choose to work with enthusiasm. It truly generates willpower to accomplish more, better, faster.

If enthusiasm is something you don't usually feel, this pre-pave will help you feel it. It works every time, if you are sincere about wanting to make a change. When you work in a state of unwillingness you get results of the same magnitude; mediocre. Unwillingness is that feeling like, "Oh darn, I have to do this now". It does not create a vibration of success around you. Change your thought immediately to one of enthusiasm and willingness to do the task. Fake it if you have to at first. You will get an instant boost of energy. Honestly, you will feel different. The moment you charge forward with enthusiasm, you receive all of the help you need to accomplish the task at hand. It gets the energy whirling in your direction. Best of all, it feels good. There is nothing more important in the Law of Attraction than feeling good. What you feel, you attract.

Nothing great was ever achieved without enthusiasm.

— Ralph Waldo Emerson

PRE-PAVE at Work

I am passionate about
what I do.

PRE-PAVE: *I am passionate about what I do.*

People often come to me for coaching on how to find a job they are passionate about. I say to them, "Be passionate about what you do now!" This is the surest way to find a job you are passionate about. You must resonate passion. Whether you are a top-paid executive or a valet, be passionate about it. When you are passionate about what you do, people notice, and so does the Universe.

A good friend of mine, Afaf Jomaa used to be a sales rep for a Canadian company with several store locations in Western Canada. Afaf's territory was all of Calgary. One day on one of her routine store visits, she noticed one of the entry-level clerks, Jane, hustling and bustling with great passion throughout the store, working as though she owned it. Afaf had noticed this about Jane's work ethic on a few occasions, but on this particular day, she had just heard word at head office that they were looking for someone to fill a corporate management position. Afaf brought Jane's name forward to the head office, with the recommendation she seriously be considered. Under normal circumstances, this young lady would never have been in the running for such a position.

Do you see how the energy of the Law of Attraction works? You do not know from where your fortune will come. You do not need to know how the Source of all abundance will reward you for your efforts. Your job is to put forth the proper thoughts, words and actions. Leave the rest to the Universe to fulfill. If you question "how", you send out a message of doubt that cancels your creation. Work like it's your own and trust.

I was totally passionate about my job as Executive Assistant to Ron Joyce. On any given week, I was on an average of four to five flights to different places, some glamorous and some not so glamorous. People would ask me, "Elisabeth, where is your favorite place to go?" I would respond, "Wherever I'm landing." I made it my choice to be passionate about wherever we were going, for whatever reason we were going there. Being passionate about what you do is a choice.

If you are a car-parker, be the best car-parker you can be.
— David Wagner

PRE-PAVE at Work

I focus on solutions today.

PRE-PAVE: *I focus on solutions today.*

I f you want to focus on problems all day, you will have a day of problems. It is your choice. If I have my choice, I choose to focus on the solutions. Wherever you put your focus, you attract the energy.

When you are unaware of the Law of Attraction, it can be so tempting to sit with colleagues and discuss everything that is wrong with the company. What if you all went back to your seats and started working on ideas for solutions, then met as a group and brainstormed your great ideas with passion? How do you think that would change the outcome of your company's success, your own success and your work environment?

Focus on solutions and the Universe will focus on getting you the resources you need. Your work environment will be far more pleasurable and you can anticipate miraculous results with this positive frame of mind.

> *Pleasure in the job puts perfection in the work.*
> *– Aristotle*

PRE-PAVE at Work

I focus on serving others.

PRE-PAVE: *I focus on serving others.*

L et's face it, whatever you do for a living, you are serving others, whether you are serving your boss, your customer or your colleague. When you focus on serving others, the Universe serves you.

Service. There is no higher purpose.

I loved being an Executive Assistant because it gave me the opportunity to serve. I adored my job. I served with passion. I tirelessly served without ever looking for anything in return. In reality, I was taken care of ten-fold.

I hear Executive Assistants talk about how they refuse to get their boss a cup of coffee. I think it's the most awesome opportunity to serve your boss. I was the one who knew best how he liked his coffee, and do you know what? There were more times than I remember that I would find my favorite iced latte on my desk waiting to surprise me after I had stepped away.

Success in life is truly about service to others and the workplace is the perfect place to practice it. Focus today on serving others. Not for what you get in return, but just for the joy of making others happy. Who knows, maybe you'll start a new trend in the office!

PRE-PAVE at Work

My meetings are successful
beyond my expectations.

PRE-PAVE: *My meetings are successful beyond my expectations.*

How often have you been anxious prior to a meeting or conference call? Anxiety is a form of worry, which is a negative pre-pave. Start each day with this pre-pave and watch your success-rate rise rapidly.

When I started my company, RnR Wellness, I began by opening the satellite spa locations before my river-front spa was built. For each new hotel I approached for the In-Room Spa, I would enter the meeting with the above pre-pave. Inevitably, I would always come out of the meeting with "wows" and "aaahs" to myself of all the unexpected great ideas that came out of the meeting that I hadn't even thought of.

When we pre-pave a specific outcome, we limit ourselves to that outcome. I urge you to pre-pave at times with open-ended success. The above pre-pave is far more powerful than pre-paving that you will "close the deal" let's say. The outcome can be so much more than just the potential partner saying yes. Why not pre-pave that they will offer further ways of partnering for success? Opportunities are limitless! Allow the Universe to work its magic by not putting limits on your success.

There might be times when you want to pre-pave a specific success and that is fine if there is something in particular that you want. At this time, the clearer you are in your goals and visualization the more successful your manifestation will be. Just be mindful of your intentions and be sure that you are in no way limiting what you accomplish.

PRE-PAVE at Work

I will shake up the world
if I have to!

PRE-PAVE: *I will shake up the world if I have to!*

This pre-pave is about perseverance. I remember building my business. In the beginning, before I had any of the hotel satellite locations, I was trying to build an on-site corporate clientele. Despite my efforts, I came up against one disappointment after another. I always kept a fantastic attitude, though. I was on a mission. With every closed door, I knew there was a far bigger and better one just down the hall. But it was at about the eighth month of starting my business that I came to a breaking point. I intuitively knew it was just a test, a test to see what I was made of. People questioned my stamina, but I persevered. It was at the moment when all others would have given up, that I said, "Okay, the gloves are off. I mean business!" I consciously decided that I would make this happen, that I would give it my 100% focus and it was sure to manifest. Within a few weeks I landed the Westin account, which continues to be my largest corporate account after several years of business.

Water can get really hot, but it takes that one extra degree to make it boil. Sometimes the Universe will test you to see if you're willing to put in that extra degree; to see if you're the one still standing to throw the last punch. Believe me, perseverance is key. No matter what the Universe is giving you at this moment in time, if you keep pursuing what you want, you will be the last one standing.

> *If you are out of a job, shake up the*
> *world until someone gives you one!*
>
> *– Paramahansa Yogananda*

PRE-PAVE at Work

I sincerely listen to my
customer.

PRE-PAVE: *I sincerely listen to my customer.*

I f you are in the service industry and most of your communication is with customers, then each time the phone rings, smile and practice this pre-pave sincerely. Each time you, yourself, place a call to a customer or enter into a meeting with a customer, practice this pre-pave. We serve our customers most effectively when we truly listen to their needs. If we supply them with things they don't need, they will be dissatisfied in the end and will take their business elsewhere. Following the Law of Attraction for success means putting energy into the Universe that will bring you back results with longevity.

Note: If you are a manager or work in Human Resources then your customer is your team-member. Whatever your position, apply this pre-pave to the people you communicate with the most. This pre-pave is about communication, which starts with "listening".

> ***No man has ever***
> ***listened himself out of a job.***
>
> — *Calvin Coolidge*

PRE-PAVE at Work

I react with kindness and
professionalism to all that
happens.

PRE-PAVE: *I react with kindness and professionalism to all that happens.*

My position with Ron Joyce was not a bed of roses. As much as I was passionate about what I was doing, in reality it was a grueling work schedule that harbored many challenges. One day, Mr. Joyce and I were speaking frankly with each other and he said to me, "No matter how hard you are crushed, you still come up smelling like a rose." That meant the world to me. It meant that I was truly living what I was studying and preparing to teach.

It matters not what happens to us. What matters is how we respond.

When an orange is squeezed, what comes out? Juice. What comes out when you are squeezed, tested or challenged? What comes out is what is inside of you. It is not the challenge that causes the reaction, it is your state of mind that causes the reaction. Your state of mind is a result of the thoughts you choose to hold.

Practice this pre-pave sincerely. Focus on reacting positively, no matter what goes on around you. No matter what others decide to do, you be the example. You be the candle that others light their candles from. When you resonate goodness against all obstacles, it will come back to you in return like a boomerang. I have proven this often in my life.

PRE-PAVE at Work

I treat this company as if
it were my own.

PRE-PAVE: *I treat this company as if it were my own.*

I always gave 100% in my position with Tim Hortons. I wasn't perfect. I made plenty of mistakes. But I always, always gave it my all. Now I own my own company. That didn't happen by chance. I attracted it to me because no matter what job I ever held, I worked like it was my own. When I worked for Ron Joyce, his company was my company. His guests were my responsibility. His family was in my care. I treated everything about his life as if it were my responsibility to make better. I focused every day on adding value to his life. I wrote those exact words in my journal daily, "I add value to Ron's life." This was a written pre-pave that came alive every day. I truly focused on it and it worked.

Try working for one day as if you owned the company. Feel how it feels to truly care about the success as an owner would. How do you think this attitude would affect your performance? People often want the perks of ownership without the elbow grease, risk and all of those things that go along with it. You may not have the desire to own your own company. I'm not saying it's for everyone. It's not. But I do know that working like you own it brings success. You resonate an energy that draws opportunity to you. If nothing else, it draws in happiness right where you are, in the job you currently do.

> *Get happiness out of your work or you may*
> *never know what happiness is.*
>
> *– Elbert Hubbard*

PRE-PAVE at Work

This is not a job;
it is a way of life.

PRE-PAVE: *This is not a job; it is a way of life.*

I f you approach your job as a way of life, you enjoy the journey, rather than watching the clock for the time you think your real life begins. I have never watched the clock in any job I've had. I've enjoyed it so much that it wasn't like work. This is something you create, not something that happens by chance because you've landed your dream job. Your dream job is now and will always be what you choose it to be.

The thoughts you hold about your job resonate around you and bring you more of what you are vibrating. Enjoy what you do as a way of life and you will reap happiness and success.

Imagine life to be a school of learning. You are in school morning, noon and night, even on weekends. Your occupation is one class of your school day, your family is another, your personal life another. If you value each part of your life as a class in a day's curriculum, including your job, you will find that going from work to home is seamless, rather than wishing all week it were Friday at five. I accomplished this in my own life by not putting a rainbow on any particular day of the week. If you live for the weekend, you will resent Monday to Friday. I always tried to look forward to each day equally.

Nothing is really work unless you would rather be doing something else.

— James M. Barrie

PRE-PAVE at Work

I follow my dreams.

PRE-PAVE: *I follow my dreams.*

I personally know that dreams come true. I had worked for Mr. Joyce for a few years before he asked me to begin traveling with him. This was a job change that would alter my life dramatically, so I went home to discuss it with my sister, Alex, whom I lived with at the time. I described the new position to her and she immediately reminded me, "Don't you remember? You dreamed this exact job!" At first I had to think about it. Then I definitely recalled having pre-paved this back when I was only 17 years of age. I remembered saying "I'm going to be Executive Assistant to a billionaire who has his own airplane." I remembered visualizing myself walking with him up to his private jet with a steno pad in my hand, taking notes as he spoke.

I knew at that moment the power of dreams and the power of one single pre-pave. This job wasn't a chance opportunity for me. I had created it in my mind, almost twenty years prior. The day the offer came in, the Universe had manifested it for me.

If you don't have a dream,
how can it come true?

PRE-PAVE at Work

It feels good to admit my
mistakes and move toward
a solution.

PRE-PAVE: *It feels good to admit my mistakes and move toward a solution.*

This pre-pave is by no means for the purpose of focusing on mistakes. Rather it focuses on honesty. There is an energy around honesty that brings you success. There is nothing like admitting your mistakes that opens up the channel for truth in any profession. What you put out you get back, remember.

Just recently, I made an error with an associate at the spa. On the surface it wasn't much, but to me it was a blunder of embarrassing proportion. I allowed myself to get frustrated with a computer glitch that was causing a bottle neck at the cash-out counter. Being anal for customer service and efficiency, I snapped at my associate when she asked me a question about the system error. It wasn't a loud snap, nor was it said with any hint of mean-ness or disrespect. After the lobby was clear, she approached me and mentioned that the customer had heard me in the office during the short exchange. I was immediately humbled and embarrassed. My initial reaction was to question how she could have heard. My next step was to justify that I didn't mean any harm with my comment, which my associate agreed. I went home that evening feeling terrible about what I had done.

Feelings are a gift, because they tell us whether we are on track or not. So I asked myself, "Why am I feeling so badly about this?" (It was really bothering me.) Was it the customer that might not have had a rosy view of me or was it my associate who I might have offended in a small way? After a little introspection, I found that what affected me the most was that I was quick to justify, quick to defend my position. I knew the spiritual danger in that type of behavior. The correct way to respond would have been to apologize, admit my error and make amends with the associate right away.

But it goes further. As I pondered everything, there was something still bothering me. I had identified the cause of my feelings and acknowledged them, but still I had a disconnect when it came to admitting I was wrong. I thought, well, I will admit my mistake to my Higher Power and that will be fine. That is sometimes all you need. In this case, I knew it wasn't good enough because I continued to struggle with my feelings. Before retiring that evening, I pre-paved that I would receive the guidance and strength necessary to make amends.

The next day, I was at the spa and found myself in a discussion with this same associate in the office. All of a sudden, I felt a wave of humility come over me. I held her by the arm to get her attention, and I sincerely apologized to her for my behavior. Tears welled up in my eyes as my whole heart was feeling the emotion of asking for sincere forgiveness. She could feel my honesty. Something was healed in that moment, for both her and me.

The next day, she admitted to some mistakes she had made that were minor but had caused some confusion with bookings. I believe she felt open enough to admit them because the day before I had fostered an environment where it would be safe to do so. I assured her that her mistakes were minor and completely salvageable (which they were). I encouraged her to keep on doing her best, that her best was awesome. A distinct shift happened that day.

If you think it is difficult to admit your mistakes, then it will continue to be so. Admitting your mistakes becomes easy when you pre-pave that it is easy. And do you see how it changes what you emit, and therefore also changes what you receive in return? When criticized or questioned about something, if you jump to defend yourself, you resonate negative energy. Instead, look within and see if what is being said is valid. If so, then work to amend your ways. If not, keep quiet and still focus on becoming better anyway. What you think and the attitude you hold toward your work, will manifest itself in some way or another, according to the nature of your thought.

PRE-PAVE at Work

I see and expect the
best in others.

PRE-PAVE: *I see and expect the best in others.*

People can feel your energy. When you think highly of them, they can feel it. When you criticize them, they can also feel it. If you are a manager, you have a profound effect on the productivity of your team. The thoughts you hold of your team will make or break your department's efficiency. It is about energy.

People become what we think of them. It is a self-fulfilling prophecy in a way, but when you understand the energy of it you will understand it more clearly. How do you feel in the presence of someone who admires you? Think of someone right now that you know feels this way about you. They feel you are professionally a "star". In their presence, you become that, don't you? **That** is energy.

The opposite is true. If you are in the presence of someone you know judges you or deems you inadequate in your job, you almost shrivel in thought when you are around this person. What happens energy-wise to your vibration is very significant. Your vibration is your magnet that creates your outer environment. The thoughts of others have a profound effect on you and your thoughts of others have a profound effect on them.

If you want to be surrounded by talented, enthusiastic people, see the best in people. Choose to focus on their talents and provide an environment for their talents to shine. You, yourself, be enthusiastic and allow your enthusiasm to inspire them to act in kind. Inspire them always to be the best they can be and show them you are there to support them.

> *We awaken in others, the attitude with which we hold toward them.*
>
> *— Elbert Hubbard*

PRE-PAVE at Work

I reward myself.

PRE-PAVE: *I reward myself.*

Regardless of position, human beings generally like acknowledgement. If we take responsibility for our own acknowledgement, we can never be disappointed. If we put this responsibility in the hands of another, we may not always be rewarded for our efforts. Knowing our thoughts create, relying on others for acknowledgement means we are putting ourselves in a position of danger when it comes to creating.

Success usually comes to those
who are too busy to be looking for it.

— Henry David Thoreau

So many times, people do good work, only to look for the pat on the back. If they don't get it right away, their energy drops. It's like planting a seed and pulling it out of the ground to see if it is growing. It will never grow if you keep pulling it up. Plant the seed of good deeds. Water it by focusing on doing more good deeds in the spirit of service.

Give yourself a pat on the back and enjoy the awesome feeling of accomplishment. If you ever get the urge to look for outside acknowledgement, focus your attention back on doing something of value. You will attract to yourself over and over again more opportunities for success. Even though you will no longer require it for fulfillment, you will receive the outside acknowledgement. Ironically, when you no longer grasp for it, it comes on its own, responding to your powerful thought.

Try not to become a man of success
but rather to become a man of value.

— Albert Einstein

PRE-PAVE at Work

Today I will make
someone's day!

PRE-PAVE: *Today I will make someone's day!*

You may deliver the mail for a living, but delivering the mail may not be your "real job" in the eyes of the Universe. It may be to connect with the elderly lady on your route who needs help picking up her newspaper from the porch. It may be the challenged boy who you uplift ever morning. These are some of the things that dictate the higher purpose of your position in life. Be open to realize these nuggets of awareness. We often get so caught up in the mundane routine of our jobs that we fail to see the big picture. We have so many opportunities throughout the day to make a difference.

A perfect example of this is described in *Life of a Daymaker*, a book written by David Wagner, a hairstylist who became a multi-millionaire partnering with the founder of Aveda. Wagner tells about how he changed the life of one of his clients who he made look beautiful one day in his hair chair. That day was a day like any other. He treated this young woman with the care and attention he did everyone. A week later, he received a letter from his client that quite changed his life. She explained that she had planned to kill herself that day. She had gone to his salon to have her hair and makeup done just right so she could feel good about herself on her last day. But after her exchange with David, and the sincere caring she felt from him, she just couldn't do it. He changed her life forever. And she changed his.

How often do we realize how much of a difference we can make in the lives of others? All it takes is a little effort, living life consciously. This pre-pave gets you there. It puts you in the mind-frame of making a difference. We get clues all of the time that there are opportunities to make a difference. What may seem insignificant at first glance, may be a charcoal cover with a diamond hidden underneath. Become aware of your true purpose. You can start by making someone's day.

> *Your work is to discover your work. Then with all your heart to give yourself to it.*
>
> *– Buddha*

PAVING IT FORWARD
in Family

PAVING IT FORWARD – IN FAMILY

My family has been a constant example of the power of pre-paving. During the early days of building my business, RnR Wellness, there were often occasions when I would work long into the evening, forgetting time. I remember calling my family to say I would be home around six p.m. Before I knew it, it was after eight o'clock. In such a circumstance you would naturally think that your family would be upset with you or resentful. The average person in my shoes would have worried on the way home which, in essence, is pre-paving a negative result.

Knowing what I know about the Law of Attraction, I pre-paved that my family would welcome me with open arms. Dinner would be ready for me. My husband and children would be understanding and supportive. And that is exactly what I would find. Call it coincidence? Most certainly not; I pre-paved it. I created it with my intention. This is the power of pre-paving in the family. What you intend, you create. Let's look at some awesome pre-paves for your family life.

PRE-PAVE in Family

My children are safe.

PRE-PAVE: *My children are safe.*

I'm a parent. I know the feeling you have where you glimpse your child hurt or in danger. It just about rips your heart out. You could travel across the room at the speed of light to catch an object that is about to fall on your child. A woman could lift a 2,000 pound car to free a child if she had to. It has happened! Where does that strength come from? These things defy logic and so does the Law of Attraction. Your thoughts can greatly affect the safety of your children.

Pre-pave every morning that they are safe. It lines up the energy for their safety. Believe it! When you kiss them as they go off to school, pre-pave their safety. Whenever you have a spare moment and you think of your children, pre-pave their safety. Visualize them surrounded in light, well taken care of, protected, happy. Think whatever positive thought makes you feel good. Your thoughts have great power. Your children will, at some level, be able to feel the protection. Hence, their safety will also be affected by the thoughts they are holding.

PRE-PAVE in Family

Today I am aware of the
non-verbal communication
from my children.

PRE-PAVE: *Today I am aware of the non-verbal communication from my children.*

S mall children communicate with us telepathically. They hear our thoughts and they are always speaking to us. Be open to this. Speak to them from your heart. Know they are hearing you. And let them know, also, that you are hearing them.

Spiritually, you can connect even more deeply when you focus on speaking to their spiritual eye, the point between the eyebrows. This is where they telepathically pick up your message and also where they speak back to you. The spiritual eye is the center of Intuition. It is also called the third eye. This center is developed when you practice meditation and yoga.

PRE-PAVE in Family

My family loves and accepts
me just as I am.

PRE-PAVE: *My family loves and accepts me just as I am.*

We tend to be more in tune with what others want for us than what we want for ourselves. As a result, we end up trying hard to please our family members rather than taking care of ourselves. Don't misunderstand the point here. Taking care of our loved ones is important, but taking care of you comes first, because you cannot take care of another person until you, yourself, are whole.

Knowing that you are loved does not make you complacent. On the contrary, when we know those around us love us deeply, it makes us want to show them our best. This is how the energy works. You can feel when others are either admiring you or criticizing you. If you could see the energy fields of two people in an exchange of criticism, it is like daggers of energy piercing into the other's vibrational field. You cannot help but feel this!

Sense how great it feels to know that your family loves and sees the best in you always.

PRE-PAVE in Family

I deeply connect with
my family.

PRE-PAVE: *I deeply connect with my family.*

The Masters of India teach that we choose our family before we arrive on this Earth, and that we are very connected with these Souls through previous lifetimes together.

I grew up in a family of six, living in southern Ontario. At the ripe age of 21, I left home and moved west to Alberta to discover life on my own. Throughout my childhood, I had always stuck close to home, even attending university in my home-town, so my sudden decision to go so far away came as a shock to everyone. As a little girl, I would even stay home from family vacations. My family would plan a vacation, and I would plan my stay-home vacation with relatives. I was very close to my grandfather and the thought of spending a week by his side was more enticing to me than spending hours in a stuffy car.

After moving west, I kept in close contact with all of my siblings but some experiences I had with my sister Alex, in particular, really helped me realize how deeply connected we are. There were times when Alex and I would not connect for a few months, not for any reason other than busy schedules. Then, out of the blue I would decide to call Alex. I would be put on hold for her at the same time a call was coming through to me. When I would pick up the other line, it would be Alex calling me, also out of the blue. This wasn't just a single occurrence. It happened often and she would vouch for me on this. Coincidence? Connection is more like it.

Then there was the time when Alex came out for a visit and we spent the weekend together reminiscing about old times and catching up on all the news. She started to relay a story and I was just about to stop her because she had told me this same story at least a dozen times before. I consciously decided not to interrupt because I noticed that she told the story with such passion. I half-listened with awe, wondering how this phenomenal, intelligent woman could not be aware of what was happening. Then a light bulb went off inside of my mind. I smiled inwardly, became present with her and listened. The key word here is just that, I **listened** to her. I listened and I heard. I heard what she said and what she didn't say. I heard what she meant, what she felt and what she wanted me to hear – for the first time. After ten kicks at the can, the Universe finally got my attention.

This incident occurred almost ten years ago now and, since then, I have not heard this story again from Alex. There was no longer a need to tell it. The story was for me, not her. Do you understand the message in this? How quickly, although briefly, did I judge the deliverer, rather than become awake enough to see the sign. The Universe had orchestrated the experience for me.

Your loved ones are your greatest teachers. Listen to them. Hear them. Deeply connect with them. Be aware of the true meaning behind these connections. Everything is always a reflection back to you, showing you the grander purpose of life.

Look into the depths of another's Soul and listen,
not only with your ears,
but with your heart and imagination,
and your silent love.

– Joye Kanelakos

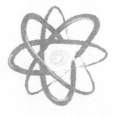

PRE-PAVE in Family

I honor my mother
and father.

PRE-PAVE: *I honor my mother and father.*

I am blessed with amazing parents. Anyone who knows me, or them, would agree. They are always there for me with hands-on support. Their service to myself and my family never stops. They do not slow down, even if they are sick, despite my sincere attempts. They are officially retired and spend their time serving their children out of the goodness of their hearts. They are a true example of selfless service. I honor them daily. A day does not pass without a feeling of deep gratitude for having such wonderful parents.

I understand that we are not all blessed with the same upbringing, but it is sad when I hear people complain about their parents. They complain about what their parents either did, or failed to do, that has apparently caused them so much grief in their lives. We are all human. We have our strengths and weaknesses. So do our parents. Being a parent is not an easy job. There is no official handbook. The importance here is to have unconditional love and respect for the people who raised you, no matter how you were raised. This counsel is included in every spiritual scripture, because it is so important.

When you harbor resentment about your parents or your childhood, you fill your vibration with negative dark clouds. You cannot expect to resonate old feelings of resentment and, at the same time, create goodness in your life. It is not vibrationally possible. Your childhood is part of your past. It does not belong to you anymore. Let it go. Do not allow any negativity to shape your today or tomorrow. Hold onto the good memories and learn the lessons from everything else.

Honor your father and mother. Extend this to your siblings, your spouse and your children. In order to attract goodness, you must fill your vibration with thoughts of goodwill to others. Start with your family, then extend those thoughts of goodwill to all.

I adore and honor my parents. Not for what they do for me, but for the great Souls that they are. My husband and I do our best in any way we can to serve them in return. We may never be able to match them, but we will certainly make it our business to keep trying.

Every minute you spend in resentment, you lose sixty seconds of peace of mind.

PAVING IT FORWARD
in Food

You cannot beat at darkness with a stick; you can only turn on the Light.

Paramahansa Yogananda

S o it is with habits and addictions. When you want to change a habit, you need to focus on the opposite quality. You bring in the Light.

Often people eat because they are bored, lonely, or simply out of habit. If this is the case for you, choose a new recreation, a new pastime, or any new sport. Sign up for some volunteer work. Take up a hobby or a yoga class. Call a friend and go for a walk in nature. Nature puts your energy field back into balance. Any of these things are great substitutes.

If you are suffering from any type of eating disorder, the pre-paves in this chapter will help to change your life from slavery to freedom. The one downside of challenges surrounding food, versus anything else, is that food is something you can't live without. Eating is a normal part of life. Your body reminds you naturally three times a day. Social gatherings revolve around food. Coffee breaks at work, meetings and romantic dates all give new reason to eat. You really can't escape it. You need to face your challenge directly and deal with it, then it will cease to trouble you.

The way you feel about food corresponds to the thoughts you have held about it. If you change your thoughts, your feelings will change and your habits will change. I have had my own personal experience with food challenges, having suffered from eating disorders for most of my twenties. I was never heavy, but was always concerned with being slim. The perception was entirely in my mind, of course, and stemmed from being in a long-term relationship that was not supportive. I know first-hand the suffering that food addiction can cause. I lived it. I believe that, somehow, I was given this experience so that I could help others. Countless people have come to me for counseling in this area, as if by magic. I love teaching that a negative tendency surrounding food can quickly become a thing of the past, if you choose it to be. It is a misconception that you need to fight temptation for the rest of your life. That goes for food, alcohol, drugs or any other addiction, including emotional addiction.

When I discovered the teachings of Paramahansa Yogananda at the age of thirty, it was like turning on a light. By focusing on absorbing the massive spiritual truths, and through the power of pre-paving, my insecurities and negative tendencies dropped within a short period of time. I didn't have to fight them. They faded away naturally. What you focus on, you create. Today, I am living proof that you can be free from addictions. I am at my ideal weight, even after just having delivered my first child. I have a healthy diet, I exercise regularly and my whole family lives a really wholesome lifestyle.

You cannot beat at darkness with a stick. You can only turn on the Light.

PRE-PAVE in Food

Bless this food.

PRE-PAVE: *Bless this food.*

I n Reiki, we learn to energize food before eating it. It changes the composition of the food and in turn, changes how effectively the nutrients are absorbed. Prayer does the same thing. When you bless your food, it spiritualizes the food, raising its vibration before it enters your body.

The vibration of what you put into your body will affect how you think, feel and behave.

PRE-PAVE in Food

I choose foods today that promote a calm state of mind.

PRE-PAVE: *I choose foods today that promote a calm state of mind.*

Most people have heard the saying, you are what you eat. The choice of the food you eat has a tremendous effect on your mood. Foods of a high vibration (fresh fruits, vegetables, nuts and grains) promote clarity, calmness and balance. Foods of a lower vibration (red meats, fast food, refined sugars and cakes) promote irritability, anger and potential health issues.

If your goal is to raise your vibration so that you are attracting health, wealth and abundance, choose foods of a high vibration. The love and care you put into the preparation of food is also a factor. Everything has a vibration. Your choice of foods, how they are prepared and how they are eaten, will significantly affect how you feel and what you will attract.

Prepare your meals with love and attention. Use the healthiest ingredients. Make mealtime special by setting the table properly or by lighting a candle. Eating on the run does not promote a calm state of mind. Make mealtime a sacred time of day. Prepare and enjoy your meals with this frame of mind for greater health and happiness.

Nothing will benefit human health and increase the chances of survival of life on Earth as much as the evolution to a vegetarian diet.

– Albert Einstein

PRE-PAVE in Food

I eat when I'm hungry and I
stop when I'm full.

PRE-PAVE: *I eat when I'm hungry and I stop when I'm full.*

Most of us, at one time or another, have experienced the discomfort of having eaten too much, such as after a big turkey dinner. Not only is it uncomfortable, it is also not good for your health. This pre-pave really helps to discourage overeating.

You can state this intention any time of day, but I suggest you repeat it again just as you sit down for a meal as well. It gets you in tune with your trigger system for hunger. It takes you away from the habit of mindless eating and helps you become a conscious and moderate eater.

Eat slowly and enjoy each morsel in mindfulness. Allow your innate trigger mechanism to kick in before you've passed the point of eating too much.

PRE-PAVE in Food

Every day I feel thinner
and thinner.

PRE-PAVE: *Every day I feel thinner and thinner.*

I frequently coach people on how to lose weight. The more you focus on your weight, the more difficult it will be to rid yourself of it. The power of affirmation lies in your belief of what you are affirming. If you affirm to yourself "I am thin" but you don't believe it or feel it on all levels, then you will actually be affirming the opposite and making it more difficult for yourself.

I recommend this pre-pave instead, "Every day I feel thinner and thinner", because it takes you one day at a time toward being thinner. Remember you can pre-pave how you want to feel. You create your body by what you are feeling or resonating. You know how great it feels when you feel thin. You're on top of the world. You feel like your weight goals are within your reach! Then the next day after you've indulged in a decadent dessert, you feel the immediate emotional effects. You spiral downward and start the roller coaster up again. What happens is that you are filling your energy field with alternately thin and heavy thoughts on these alternating days. You swing your vibration back and forth, and that stops you from moving forward in a positive direction.

Pre-pave how you want to feel. When you feel thin, you will naturally choose healthy foods, foods that will keep you thin. Your feelings will support healthy actions.

It is important here to mention that I am not suggesting thin is better. Whatever makes you feel good is best. I mention "thin" only for those who wish to lose weight. It is the best method I have found in coaching people to shift their consciousness toward reaching their weight goals.

PRE-PAVE in Food

Today I eat my meals in silence.

PRE-PAVE: *Today I eat my meals in silence.*

In most ashrams and monasteries, meals are eaten in silence. In the Buddhist tradition, it is taught that when you are eating, you do nothing else but eat. You focus on the food. You focus on what you are doing.

In the Hindu tradition, silence is also practiced, with observance of the in-dwelling Spirit. A young boy was living in the YSS School for Boys in Ranchi, India, founded by Paramahansa Yogananda. He was there all summer learning techniques of mindfulness, meditation and spiritual living. In this boys' school, parents are only allowed to visit once in a while, to give the boys a chance to totally immerse themselves in the spiritual teachings. One day, the mother of this particular young boy came to join him for lunch. As they were enjoying a simple lunch outside on the grounds on a beautiful day, the mother tried continuously to get the boy's attention. Despite repeated attempts, he didn't respond, as though he couldn't hear her. When she questioned him as to why he wasn't responding, he quietly said "Mother, I like to think of God while I eat this food."

The Masters of India teach a focus on God while eating. I realize eating in silence isn't always possible in today's modern world with breakfast, lunch and dinner meetings being a way of the usual business regime. But if you can practice it even sometimes, you will find a positive change in your thought patterns and eating habits. Taste the food. Feel it going down to the stomach. Intend that it nourish you and bring you good health.

When you eat in silence, your body naturally will eat only what you need and no more, and you will reap the most nutrition possible from the food. Eating in silence, or doing anything in silence, is also an avenue to strengthen your Intuition.

PAVING IT FORWARD
at Night

Once again, it bears reminding that first thing in the morning and last thing at night are the two most powerful times of the day to pre-pave. As your consciousness is drifting into and out of the sub-conscious state, the energy for creating is most acute.

The only time you are not creating or manifesting is when your conscious mind is completely asleep. It is important for you to know, however, that the sub-conscious mind never sleeps. It is always awake. It is always absorbing what is going on around you as you sleep. So I caution you against falling asleep to the nightly news or anything that might put negativity into your consciousness. Despite the fact that your conscious mind is asleep, your sub-conscious mind will absorb anything it hears and will program itself accordingly.

Your sub-conscious mind holds within itself your entire belief system. Whatever you program into it, whether awake or asleep, will affect what you attract and create during the day. But do not confuse this outside stimuli with dreams. You do not create from your dreams, unless you bring your dream thoughts into your waking consciousness during the day. This is discussed in greater detail later on in this chapter.

To help you understand the power of night-time pre-paves, I will share with you my first experience of meditation. It was during a weekend course that I attended in Calgary called Spectra, led by a Calgary woman named Diane Cox. If I had known it was a course in meditation at the time I would not have attended. I had no interest in meditation. I didn't know what it was. I had just turned thirty and was going through a major relationship break-up with a man I had shared the prior ten years of my life with. We owned homes, businesses and dogs together, luckily no children. The separation shook up my life to say the least. Diane's son, Jeffrey, was a good friend of mine at the time and he urged me to take his mother's series of classes. Jeffrey was always talking about the "energy" of things and it used to spook me because it was foreign. Often, what we don't understand we dismiss as false or impossible. His continuous talk of "energy" was one of those things for me and I assumed his mother would be talking the same language, so I had my apprehensions. I ended up going ahead anyway and attended the weekend course, knowing nothing of what I was in for.

The weekend changed my life. It was the beginning, for me, of a new way of thinking. The course included an introduction to meditation, but more so, delved into positive programming of the sub-conscious mind. There were passages we were given to read and we were to practice reading them just before going to sleep. These passages were positive paragraphs to program the sub-conscious mind for success and happiness. The way I would explain them now is that they were paragraphs of positive pre-paves.

It was during that weekend that I was also introduced to a book written by Paramahansa Yogananda, titled *Where There Is Light*. It was this book that piqued my interest enough to dive further into Eastern philosophy and the study of energy, which have so fueled my life over the past two decades and have guided me to inspire thousands of others with the message. In summary, this weekend course I was initially reluctant to take ended up making, perhaps, the most significant impact in the course of my life.

Upon awakening, and just before sleep are the most important times to positively pre-pave.

I have explained to you already the method of a hypnotist. When you pre-pave, you are giving the sub-conscious mind a command. It takes it as truth and begins to manifest it. In the morning and at night, when your conscious and sub-conscious minds are alternately disconnecting and connecting with each other again, these are the two most powerful times for programming positive pre-paves into your sub-conscious mind.

Turn your worries, anxieties and fears into positive nightly pre-paves. In time, the thoughts you roll around in your mind as you fall asleep and as you wake up, will naturally be positive, creating good things for you always. As a Reiki Master, with a keen sense of energy, I understand this in my heart on all levels. I hope that I have explained this in terms you can understand and follow. If you are still not convinced, test it for yourself and discover your own magnified power at this time of day.

PRE-PAVE at Night

I pre-pave a restful sleep.

PRE-PAVE: *I pre-pave a restful sleep.*

When I was fifteen years old, my sister, Mary and I planned an impromptu trip to Florida during our spring break. The only flight we could get was one that departed out of the Toronto airport at six o'clock in the morning, which meant we had to get up at three a.m. in order to catch the flight. That night, we told ourselves we had to wake up! We set our alarm, but inadvertently set the alarm for three p.m. instead of three a.m. Despite no alarm, and no previous pattern of waking up in the middle of the night, we both magically woke up just within minutes of three a.m., wondering why the alarm didn't ring.

We had pre-paved the night before that we would wake up at that particular time, and our bodies woke us up without the alarm. Everyone has proven this at one time or another. This is how pre-paving works. Never under-estimate the power of your thoughts in the creation process. If you tell your body at night to wake you up at a certain time, it will. So it goes with pre-paving a restful sleep. The Universe makes it happen according to your demand. Believe in your power.

PRE-PAVE at Night

Tonight I will fall asleep quickly and sleep right through the night.

PRE-PAVE: *Tonight I will fall asleep quickly and sleep right through the night.*

I f you suffer from insomnia, this is the pre-pave you can practice in order to change to a better sleep pattern. Tell yourself you will have a restful sleep and that you will fall asleep quickly. Pre-pave whatever you want. Your body will follow suit.

Your creative energy is very strong at night and it will create what you consciously or unconsciously intend. If you anticipate insomnia, insomnia is what you will create. If you pre-pave the opposite, and believe it, you will be able to enjoy the sleep you so need and deserve.

Sleep is very important to the body and mind to rejuvenate. You need this rejuvenation. The Universe wants to give it to you. It is just waiting for your command.

> *There is a time for many words.*
> *And there is also a time for sleep.*
>
> *– Homer (700 BC) The Odyssey*

PRE-PAVE at Night

I receive important messages
in my dreams.

PRE-PAVE: *I receive important messages in my dreams.*

When we are in the dream state, this is the one time that we are not creating, or changing our destiny. We could be having dreams of wealth, or dreams of living on the street, but neither would change our outer circumstance. The only way in which our dreams can manifest outwardly is if we carry our dreams into our conscious thoughts during the day. In other words, if you have a bad dream and wake up thinking about it throughout the day, then you are negatively creating as you put negative thoughts into your vibration. The key is to release any negativity from your dreams so as not to manifest negativity in your life. Receive the message. Learn the lesson. Release the rest.

Dreams provide us with messages. When you wake up and recall a dream you've had, instantly ask yourself, "What did it mean? What was it trying to tell me?" The answer that comes immediately to you is the lesson you are supposed to take from it. By practicing this technique, you will know when your Intuition is speaking to you clearly.

If you want to strengthen your Intuition in general, or you wish to receive a specific answer to a question, you can ask to have the answer brought to you in a dream by writing it down. Write the question beside your bed and ask that the answer come to you during the night. When you awake and the message is clear, write down your thoughts immediately so you can capture them in their purity. I caution against reading the significance of dreams in a dream dictionary unless you feel strongly compelled. A better technique is the one I have described above.

I will help to clarify this with a quick lesson in energy. You have seven energy centers in your body. Imagine them appearing as funnels filled with light, vibrating and changing according to your thought. If you go outside of yourself for answers, the energy center of Intuition located near your forehead closes up. When you wake up and a dream is fresh in your mind, your Intuition will tell you immediately what the lesson or message was. If you have to analyze it or get the mind involved, the message can become unclear. Your Intuition is always the **first** thought that comes to mind. Use it to guide you, not just in analyzing dreams, but in all areas of your life.

PRE-PAVE at Night

I dream dreams of beauty and
happy experiences.

PRE-PAVE: *I dream dreams of beauty and happy experiences.*

Your dream state is actually a reflection of the state of your sub-conscious mind. Dreams are meant for your enjoyment, but at the same time, they are usually telling you something.

If you have been suffering from nightmares, this is a good pre-pave because you are telling the Universe what kind of dreams you want to have.

> *Imagine all the people living in peace.*
> *You may say I'm a dreamer but*
> *I'm not the only one.*
> *I hope someday you'll join us,*
> *and the world will live as One.*
>
> *– John Lennon*

PRE-PAVE at Night

I am conscious in my dreams.

PRE-PAVE: *I am conscious in my dreams.*

Just as you can create your waking experiences, you can create your dreams. Visualize what kind of dreams you want to have and pre-pave that you will be conscious in them. That is, you can consciously decide right in the dream where you want to go with the plot, knowing full well that it is only a dream. This is an opportunity to have some fun!

I am personally a very vivid dreamer. I know everyone isn't like this. My husband doesn't dream at all, ever, or at least doesn't recall that he does. To me, it feels like I dream continuously throughout the night. I have had so much fun consciously creating my dreams over the years. I love it. It's exciting. I can be skiing in the Swiss Alps one night and riding the San Diego surf the next. It's like a great escape from life. In my dreams I can do things I don't do in my waking life. And when I wake up, I feel like I've been on vacation.

Some men see things as they are and say 'Why?'
I dream of things that never were and say 'Why not?'

– George Bernard Shaw

PRE-PAVE at Night

I honestly and sincerely
review the day.

PRE-PAVE: *I honestly and sincerely review the day.*

Night-time introspection is critical for self-improvement. Run through the events of the day in your mind. Use them to learn. If you want to change the energy of something that happened, replay it in your mind with a different outcome. If you didn't like your behavior, change your response as you play it back, or change the feeling to one you wish you would have had. This changes the energy of it to the positive and can help you go forward with good thoughts about every situation. You can heal anything from the past by bringing it into the present and intending a change. This is a great way to mend relationships or anything that needs healing.

The purpose of introspection is to guide you to becoming the person you want to be. It also strengthens your Intuition which is so important in consciously creating. If you let a horse run loose, unattended, it may run wild. So it is with our behavior and tendencies. We must reel them in nightly to keep ourselves on track. Look at yourself honestly and whatever habits you want to adopt or circumstances you want to create, pre-pave them now, at the most creative time of day, just before you fall asleep.

The unexamined life is not worth living.

– Socrates

PRE-PAVE at Night

I pray for others.

PRE-PAVE: *I pray for others.*

You are a powerful creator at night, so use this time to pray for others. It is a great habit to get into. You will always be able to think of someone in your life who needs help. And if you can't think of anyone, then pray for world peace. What if each person on Earth prayed for world peace each night for one minute? Imagine how that would change the world.

I had the privilege of hearing Marianne Williamson speak recently in Calgary. She delivered a powerful message. She said, "To all of you who think you can't do anything to save people in a far-off country, believing that perhaps it's just their karma, I challenge you to deem it your karma to do something about it!" I applaud Marianne for saying it so profoundly. I will add to her words and say this: "The best way to start is with prayer." Miracles happen with prayer. Do your part in making a global change by spending one minute in prayer each night. If you could see the energy of prayer, you would see light leaving your third eye to surround the person for whom you are praying. You can make a difference in another part of the world by visualizing a whole country immersed in light. The power of prayer is phenomenal.

> *One determined person can make a significant difference. A small group of determined people can change the course of history.*
>
> *– Sonia Johnson*

PRE-PAVE at Night

I am grateful for _____.

PRE-PAVE: *I am grateful for* _____.

As you are falling asleep, this is a great time to think of all of the things you are grateful for. Instead of counting sheep, count your blessings. It feels great. Your energy automatically changes. It relaxes you and helps you sleep.

Of all of the nightly pre-paves, the best to end with are Prayer and Gratitude; the reason they are the last pre-paves of this chapter. Make them a nightly habit so they become automatic. If you do, you will find that if you awake throughout the night, your mind will immediately return there. These thoughts have the power to create at a magnified frequency. Use them to create goodness for yourself and others. If you leave your mind to chance at night, you could wind up in thoughts of worry. Re-program your mind with pre-paving so it automatically goes to the positive. Your thoughts during the night are truly a reflection of where your mind has been all day, especially just before you fall asleep.

When I go on spiritual retreat, I find myself waking in the middle of the night with spiritual chants* in my mind from the evening's meditation. How beautiful it feels to wake up with such high vibrational thoughts rolling through my consciousness, so automatically and naturally. The goal is to live in this high vibration always. Through pre-paving, morning and night, and all through the day, this high state of consciousness is possible. It becomes not just a habit, but a way of life.

It is a sign of mediocrity,
when you demonstrate gratitude with moderation.

– Robert Benigni

---

*Chanting is a form of devotional prayer with melody that helps the mind to focus on the object of concentration, God.

PAVING IT FORWARD
in Love

PAVING IT FORWARD – IN LOVE

This chapter is about relationships of every kind, not just those of a romantic nature. Relationships are always about two things: You and Love. The common denominator is You and the lesson is about unconditional Love. You can guide yourself in any relationship by asking yourself "What would Love do?" Looking beyond the surface of the exterior, rising above the obvious, you discover the true meaning behind every exchange. Our friends, siblings and Soul mates are our greatest teachers.

The meeting of two personalities is like the contact of two chemical substances; if there is any reaction, both are transformed.

– Carl Jung

PRE-PAVE in Love

I treat myself with respect,
patience and understanding.

PRE-PAVE: *I treat myself with respect, patience and understanding.*

The first relationship we have is with ourselves. This relationship sets the tone for all other relationships. We teach people how to treat us. How we treat ourselves, eventually manifests in our relationships with others. We start a trend of healthy relationships with others by treating ourselves with the kindness and love with which we wish others would treat us.

Focus today on seeing your own goodness. Be gentle and kind with yourself. The way you wish to be treated, treat yourself in this way. Focus on loving yourself in a way that you would ultimately like to be loved by another.

Hate the sin. Love the sinner.

– Mahatma Gandhi

PRE-PAVE in Love

Today I heal one relationship
in my life.

PRE-PAVE: *Today I heal one relationship in my life.*

This is meant to be directed toward anyone with whom you have challenges or anyone close in your life where you, at some point, might have had difficulties. It can be someone who is alive, or someone who has passed on. It can even be yourself. We all have relationships that need healing. Today, choose the one that stands out for you to be the most significant relationship to heal at this time, then begin following these steps.

1. Set your intention to heal your relationship with this person.

2. Forgive them for something they have done or failed to do, anything that you might be holding onto.

3. Focus on one or two good qualities that they have; traits you admire about them.

4. We are all One, and we all have the same need for happiness, we just choose to express it in different ways. Acknowledge their connection to you and accept their uniqueness.

5. Say a prayer for them or send them a powerful good wish.

6. Thank the Universe, for the healing has already begun and will continue all day.

7. Lastly, perform a random act of kindness. If this person is alive and close in proximity to you, do or say something sincerely nice for them within the next 24 hours. If this person is far away or has passed on, you can do much with just a thought.

This process is very powerful when you are sincere about your intention. Relationships connect us to Spirit and, when we are in harmony with others, our connection to Spirit is greatly deepened. It is in our very best interest to work on healing our relationships regularly. Relationships are our greatest teachers.

> *You can make more friends in two months by becoming interested in other people than you can in two years by trying to get other people interested in you.*
> *– Dale Carnegie*

PRE-PAVE in Love

We greet each other with respect.

PRE-PAVE: *We greet each other with respect.*

Think of this typical scenario: A wife has been cooped up in the house all day with her children and their demands. She looks forward to her husband's arrival home so she can pass off the children to him for a while, giving herself a break, as though he's been on vacation all day. The husband coming home to this scenario has had a challenging day himself. He can only respond by dumping his own garbage onto his wife and children, as he unloads his own burden of the day.

In India, it is customary for the wife to bathe and dress herself and the children for her husband's arrival home from work each day. You can bet that with this greeting, the husband does not dump his challenges onto his family. Rather, he puts them aside and receives them as they have received him, like royalty. What a beautiful custom!

I, personally, have a thing about how couples greet each other. I think it sets the tone of respect in the house. If my husband or I leave the house just to go down to the corner store, we find each other in the house, wherever we might be, and we give each other a kiss. Upon our return, we find each other again in the house and repeat the romantic gesture. In this way, we show respect for each other.

When one of us comes home after a long day, the first thing we do is find each other in the house and give each other a greeting as though we hadn't seen each other in days. No matter what life threw us today, we're now home and safe in the presence of someone who loves us.

This kind of respectful behavior does so much for a relationship! It took time to cultivate this habit. One day, early on in our relationship, Anton came right out onto the lawn to greet me as he saw my car pulling up toward the house. I exclaimed "This is what I mean! How beautiful is this!" At first, he didn't see the value in such a greeting. He even joked that if he were to greet me in this way every day, I would come to expect it. To this day, he either understands my way of thinking, or he plays along to make me happy. Either way, it doesn't matter to me because I'm getting what I want, a relationship based on respect. Why not expect the best, and live up to the best? Do you want a mediocre relationship or a phenomenal one?

Respect yourself and others will respect you.

– Confucious

PRE-PAVE in Love

Today I release the past.

PRE-PAVE: *Today I release the past.*

Just as much as we wish our loved ones would release the negativity from the past, we too must release any negativity that we might be holding onto. Whatever you keep bringing into your thoughts today from the past you put into your vibrational field today, creating your present and future.

Don't hang on to things your friend or partner might have said that hurt your feelings days ago. Let it go. Whatever you focus on, the Universe brings to you. When you start to resonate what you want in a relationship, it is already being created.

Do not associate yourself with temporary flashes of error.

— Paramahansa Yogananda

PRE-PAVE in Love

I release relationships
that no longer serve me.

PRE-PAVE: *I release relationships that no longer serve me.*

Relationships sometimes run their course and serve their purpose in a specified period of time. There will be circumstances in your life when relationships are better to end and this is more than okay. Often, the reason we stay longer than necessary in a relationship is due to fear. We don't feel good enough about ourselves in order to leave. Low self-esteem has a great impact on our relationships.

Difficult decisions are tough, yes, but you learn from each difficult experience. When your Intuition tells you something is over and you continue to stay, it is like running into a brick wall. Each time you get the message to go, but you stay, is like running at the wall with a little more speed. Eventually, you get going fast enough and the blow hits you hard enough to get your attention.

You don't have to let it get to that point. Take care of yourself. Listen to your feelings. Tune in to your Intuition. It is always speaking to you. You will know in your heart what serves you and what does not. Have the courage to release what needs to be released when the time is right. Sometimes, it doesn't mean to release the entire relationship, merely a pattern in the relationship. Be aware of that; things on the outside change when we change things on the inside. Even others change when we change ourselves inside.

PRE-PAVE in Love

I show my true self to others.

PRE-PAVE: *I show my true self to others.*

We are good at hiding ourselves very carefully from others. How can they love us if we don't allow them in? Relationships need us to be "real". Focus on being "real" today with others. A little vulnerability is necessary, sometimes, to let go of the layers that have covered you. Do not think vulnerability is a bad thing. You can feel good about showing your true self to others by pre-paving that you are safe in doing so. Pre-pave that your heart is in good hands and it will be. You are creating your relationship as you go, with your thoughts.

> *A friend is one before whom I may think aloud.*
>
> *– Ralph Waldo Emerson*

PRE-PAVE in Love

I am special. I appreciate my
own uniqueness.

PRE-PAVE: *I am special. I appreciate my own uniqueness.*

Only You can provide the Universe with the unique expression of You.

It is common for people to compare themselves to those around them, thinking perhaps this person has more of something than they have. Unless you walk in that person's shoes, you have no idea what they have in their life. Do not envy anyone. Do not wish to be anyone else, or to have the life of anyone else. It puts envy into your vibrational field and you attract people that are envious or you attract circumstances to spark more envy. Your mind is your greatest asset. You do not know what goes through the minds of others so never envy another.

If you see a trait in someone that you admire, use the power of your mind to adopt that trait. If you see someone owning something you wish to own, pre-pave it into existence for yourself and act in accordance with your desire.

PRE-PAVE in Love

I see myself honestly.

PRE-PAVE: *I see myself honestly.*

We are often quick to judge others, but slow to be honest with the things about ourselves that we would like to change. Focus on yourself today. Those things you want to change about yourself, acknowledge them and change them. Be honest with who you are and where you want to go with your life.

PRE-PAVE in Love

Today I see the best in others.

PRE-PAVE: *Today I see the best in others.*

> When you look for the best in others, you find the best in yourself.

No matter how much a person might irritate you, you can always find something good about them. Whatever you look for, you will find.

Let's go further on this and discuss the energy of this concept. This is very important. Whatever quality you detect in another, you would not see if it did not, on some level or to some degree, resonate within yourself. Yes, this is true; it is how energy works.

PRE-PAVE in Love

Today I focus on
understanding others.

PRE-PAVE: *Today I focus on understanding others.*

I f you want your relationships to change for the better, practice this pre-pave and really mean it. When you are stuck in the attitude of feeling misunderstood or desperately trying to be heard, your energy vibrates it so loudly that it creates a gap between you and them. You are over here wanting to be understood, and they are over there wanting to be understood. The only way you bridge the gap is if one person backs down and reaches out to the other in understanding. What does it matter who that person is, as long as the gap is bridged? Take control of your life. You be that person who focuses on understanding.

> *You be the candle that others light*
> *their candles from.*
>
> *— Dennis Weaver*

PRE-PAVE in Love

Whatever I want out of a
relationship, I focus on giving it.

PRE-PAVE: *Whatever I want out of a relationship, I focus on giving it.*

When you ask yourself, "How do I feel?" you are consciously checking in to see if your thoughts are currently on track. Any negative emotion you feel in a relationship is actually a blessing. It is a sign that your thoughts are not taking you in the direction you want the relationship to go. When you check in with your feelings and you find that they are negative, take this opportunity to change your thought immediately. You do this by asking yourself the second question, "What do I want out of the relationship?" When you identify what you want, you can focus your attention in that right direction. You will find that your feelings will follow suit.

For example, if you are feeling sad and you realize that it is because you feel you are not getting enough love from your partner, pre-pave that love is your goal. Say to yourself, "I want love in my life!" Then focus on giving love. Focus on friendship. Be a friend to your partner. You will resonate friendship and caring, and it will be returned to you.

The moment you pre-pave, the Universe starts immediately to create it. To make it more powerful, hold the thought with sustained effort and feel gratitude that it is already being created. Sometimes, there is a tendency to pull away when you don't feel loved, but this will give you the opposite of what you seek.

I have the most incredible husband. His love, generosity and consideration go way beyond my expectations, daily. And I have high standards. Anton is nothing less than extraordinary in every way. I would not be here writing this book if it were not for his love, support and continuous inspiration. It took me close to forty years to find him, but he was worth the wait. I know how lucky I am to have him in my life and I tell him often. He usually agrees with me, which is part of his wonderful sense of humor.

One day, I was feeling unloved. I wasn't getting the usual affection and attention from Anton that I was accustomed to. I felt the urge to pull away and part of me did, despite my attempts to keep my thoughts on a high plane. I had a sad feeling in the pit of my stomach all evening and went to bed with the same feeling. His withdrawn demeanor lasted a few days. I couldn't help but be affected by it, because I had allowed my own vibration to sink.

A few days later, we were casually talking and he confessed to me that he had been suffering from a severe headache the past few days and it had finally ceased. He hadn't said anything earlier because he didn't want to burden me with it. What a huge lesson I learned that day. I had withdrawn from him at a time when he needed me the most. When he was suffering, I should have given him understanding, care and comfort. Instead I wallowed in my own insecurity of why I wasn't receiving love. I learned that day the power of receiving what you want out of a relationship by giving it.

There is no remedy for love but to love more.

– Henry David Thoreau

PRE-PAVE in Love

I am that which I am, and I
allow others to be as they are.

PRE-PAVE: *I am that which I am, and I allow others to be as they are.*

> The Law of Allowing: I am that which I am, and I allow others to be as they are.

This is more than just a pre-pave. In relationships, this is the key to keeping your own vibration high. It is what is known as "The Law of Allowing" and carries within it a stick of dynamite. It means that no matter what someone is doing outside of you, you still remain happy within.

Adhering to the Law of Allowing does not make you a doormat, nor does it make you demean yourself in any way by accepting inappropriate behavior from another person. What it does mean, is that nothing another person does or says has the ability to upset your state of consciousness, your inner peace of mind or your happiness.

The Masters of India teach that even-mindedness is the most important quality to strive for. We need to practice even-mindedness in our relationships; not flying off the handle when someone does something that irritates us or hurts our feelings. In fact, if you were truly following the Law of Allowing, then you could never feel hurt or irritated due to the speech or actions of another. No one can offend you without your permission.

Wayne Dyer tells a great story about when he was on the road speaking. He had very little time to exercise one day and so when he checked into his hotel, he put on his sneakers. He took a ten-minute opportunity to run up and down the hallway to get a little bit of exercise before his evening speaking engagement. One lady, checking into her room at the time, was openly disgusted with his behavior in the hallway. After she checked into her room, she kept opening her door and making comments and gestures reflecting her feelings about it. His actions had nothing to do with her! She was creating negativity in her own vibrational field because of something that was going on outside of her.

How often do we do this, with our colleagues, our children, our spouse? Think about it. What another person does is truly none of your business when it comes to allowing it to upset you or rob you of your happiness. It doesn't mean you do not deal with issues that affect you. On the contrary, but you deal with them with a frame of mind that focuses on the outcome that you want to achieve. That is practicing the Law of Allowing.

Remember this; the purpose of pre-paving is to "raise your vibration" because the Law of Attraction is always at work. You attract what you vibrate. By following The Law of Allowing, you keep that vibration high. We are in a continuous string of relationships, at work, at home, in social settings, everywhere! It is the one thing we cannot escape in this world, relating with others. When we can successfully follow the Law of Allowing, we keep our vibration high. There is nothing more important than feeling good in the Law of Attraction. Feeling good is the goal of pre-paving.

When you change the way you look at things,
the things you look at change.

– Wayne Dyer

PRE-PAVE in Love

Today I keep my vibration high
and uplift others around me.

PRE-PAVE: *Today I keep my vibration high and uplift others around me.*

Let's talk about the energy of interaction. If you could see the energy fields of two people in an exchange, you would see the reason behind keeping your own vibration high. To keep your own vibration high means to fill your energy field with positive and uplifting thoughts only. You do this by positively pre-paving.

When you mix with others, your energy field is greatly affected. We have all felt the feeling of being drained by another person. It is the feeling that someone has sucked your energy dry. This is not just a feeling. It is what really happens. If you put positive and negative thoughts into your vibration, you become a mediocre magnet. This magnet is vulnerable to the influence of others around you. In this state, when you come into contact with a positive person, you are uplifted. When you come into contact with a negative individual, your energy is depleted. This is why you feel drained. There is no magic to it. It is energy and it is always working.

When you keep your thoughts always positive by pre-paving every part of your day, you become a super-charged, positive magnet. Anyone who comes into your realm will either be repelled or uplifted by your presence. Here is an example of someone being repelled: in a high vibrational state, you enter into a conversation with someone of a low vibration. Within a few moments the conversation ends abruptly. Your friend excuses himself. He is not even sure why, he just has to go. Another example might be this: you are on your way to the lunch room at work and a negative person is in the lunch room. All of a sudden you get the urge to go to the café around the corner for lunch instead. You miss him entirely. Energy is a very powerful thing. Do not under-estimate it.

Do you see the importance of keeping your vibration high? Do you understand how it affects your relationships?

We need to keep this in mind when others come to us for comfort. I coach people very pointedly on this topic. Someone may come to you in dire need of advice, suffering from a bad relationship or an abusive spouse perhaps. A common mistake is to add fuel to the fire by saying, "What a monster! How terrible! How could he or she do this to you?" This does no good, neither for you nor the person suffering.

If you lower your vibration by getting emotional with them or by stoking the flame, you cannot expect to uplift them. It is not vibrationally possible. In any such exchange, focus on keeping your thoughts positive. This is the way to keep your own vibration high. Focus on helping the person find, within themselves, the answers they need to find from the experience. You do not know why their karma has brought them to this point, nor the life lesson they are to learn from it. All you can do is help them see the good in themselves. Guide them to tune in to their own Intuition for the answers they need. Just by being of a high vibration and allowing them to speak will heal them, without you even saying a word. I have done this countless times. I have received calls from people as they are driving away from me saying, "Thank you so much, you have healed me". I barely said a word. I listened. I kept my own thoughts on a high plane. I visualized them surrounded in light. I pictured them as I knew they would want to feel, live and be. I trusted that they would be well. That is it.

> *If you truly care about others, you will keep yourself in a high vibrational state when you mix with them. That is true Compassion.*

A woman who was consoling a friend who had come to her in grief about an abusive husband questioned me on this. "But how is that being a good friend if I don't feel her pain and express my utter disgust with what this man has done to her? That is the opposite of compassion!" To her I responded, "If you truly care about your friend, you will keep yourself in a high vibrational state when you mix with her. You will spark her to look within herself rather than to you as a guiding light. Yes, you can validate her feelings and yes, you can acknowledge her current situation. But you will not wallow, nor will you stoop, to criticize her husband. You will pray for both her and her husband. He needs it the most! You will always help her to see the positive in her life. You will help her to find the strength to make difficult decisions. (You don't have that strength with a lowered vibration!) You will help her focus on the positive traits of her husband. You will remind her of the power of prayer. You will urge her to focus on learning the lesson buried within the challenge and to find the gift that lies within it. That is the true way of compassion."

PRE-PAVE in Love

I approach all others today
with compassion.

PRE-PAVE: *I approach all others today with compassion.*

Compassion is something that is a major focus of the Buddhist teachings. Compassion is to acknowledge that we are essentially One and that we all seek the same two things:

1. Happiness
2. To be free of suffering.

We may express our needs in different ways, but in essence, all human beings are equal in this regard. If you were to approach every exchange you had with another person with compassion, how would this change the quality of your relationships?

If someone were to act inappropriately, rather than judge this person, practice compassion. Start by asking for understanding. Acknowledge that they are seeking the same things you are. Ask yourself how you can you help them find happiness and help them free themselves from suffering.

Imagine how different life would be if everyone approached each other from a place of compassion.

> *The purpose of our lives is to be happy.*
>
> *– Dalai Lama*

PAVING IT FORWARD
in Creating

W ithout a doubt, there is a formula for creating. For those of you who like a recipe, here you go; follow this mix. It is a proven method in which you can day by day move your energy toward manifesting what you want. It is called *The Law of Deliberate Creation*. It states that what you manifest, is based on two things:

Desire and Belief

50% what you desire or think about,
50% what you believe you can have.

In other words, when you desire something strongly (therefore focusing on it always) and you believe you can have it, it will manifest.

In theory, this may seem a little simplistic. Creating is simple! But let us expand on the formula. It first takes **Intuition** to know what you want. Otherwise, there is a tendency for thoughts to waiver from this to that. Another tendency is to focus on the lack of what you want, if that is your current situation. These are two very common thought patterns that are addressed in the following pages.

Once you know what you want, and you begin to focus your thoughts in that direction, the next step is to ensure that your internal belief system supports your desires. The best (and easiest) way is through pre-paving. Each positive pre-pave programs the sub-conscious mind to believe that you already have what you want.

But then you must act. You can't sit on the couch eating potato chips expecting your goals to happen. It's like hoping to win the lottery without buying a ticket. When you act, you move the energy forward in the direction you want to go. Like raising one hand, the Divine lowers two to pick you up. Like putting money into an investment plan, the Universe matches your investment. Pre-paving is your first form of action. By pre-paving, you make a command and a commitment to follow through on your good intentions. Pre-paving also raises your vibration, which puts you into alignment with what you want to receive.

In essence then, the steps to Conscious Creating are this:

1. Intuition: Being clear on what you want.

2. Desire: Unwavering focus on what you want.

3. Belief: Matching your beliefs with your desires.

4. Action: Making a move and paving it forward.

The pre-paves that follow will help you develop in all of these areas of Conscious Creation.

PRE-PAVE in Creating

Today I spend some time in
Silence.

PRE-PAVE: *Today I spend some time in Silence.*

> *Seclusion is the price of greatness.*
>
> *— Paramahansa Yogananda*

W hy do you think the great Masters of India spent years in the Himalayas?

If you have never consciously spent time in silence, take some time today. A starting point may be to just turn off the radio or television for a while. Later, try truly being silent, which means to silence the thoughts, even if only for thirty minutes or so.

Look ahead and see if there is a time where you could take a whole day, or even a week and attend a silent retreat. I have spent the last two decades going to numerous retreats. My usual destination is an ocean-side Ashram in Encinitas, near San Diego. Sometimes, I go to winter destinations in the mountains of Alberta. Where you go doesn't matter, but if you can, choose a place of breathtaking natural beauty. It helps to foster a change in consciousness. The energy of Mother Nature puts you in immediate balance. Your energy changes the moment you look out into the depths of the ocean or get lost in the vastness of a mountain range.

In order to discover yourself and what you want out of life, you must be prepared to spend some time with yourself, alone, in silence.

> *In the attitude of Silence, the Soul finds the path in a clearer light. What is elusive and deceptive resolves itself into crystal clearness.*
>
> *Our life is a long and arduous quest after Truth.*
>
> *— Mahatma Gandhi*

PRE-PAVE in Creating

I follow my Intuition.

PRE-PAVE: *I follow my Intuition.*

If you can cultivate a strong Intuition, you can become a powerful creator in every avenue of life. One of the most common mistakes is to continuously sway your thoughts from one thing to the next saying, "I want this. No, I want that". You end up sending out mixed messages and end up right back where you started. By cultivating a strong Intuition, you save a lot of time and energy.

There are distinct ways you can use energy to strengthen your Intuition. As previously mentioned, the energy center in the body that governs Intuition is located at the point between the eyebrows. Imagine it to be a funnel of energy facing out the front of your forehead and out the back of your head. All of the answers you need to know in your life are right within you. This is what your Intuition is. It is an inner knowing of what feels good. No one else knows what is best for you. You know what is best. When you seek answers to life's important questions outside of yourself, the energy center in your forehead diminishes and shuts down. Your Intuition says, "Close it down boys, we're not needed right now!" When you focus within for answers with a feeling of trust, this funnel of energy becomes vibrant and wide, and the answers begin to flow freely.

I learned my greatest lesson about Intuition in one single experience that changed my life forever. In my mid-thirties, I found myself at a cross-road in my life, with some big decisions to make. Great opportunities were being presented to me and I wanted to be sure I was making the right choices, as they would seriously affect my destiny. I kept asking myself, "What should I do?" Both roads were great choices, but for the life of me, I could not figure out which road was the best to take.

I ended up in a room full of Reiki Masters one evening. One lady was a practicing psychic as well. She and I spoke briefly during the break, and I told her about my dilemma. She offered to read my future, which I happily accepted. Let me first qualify the process of what a psychic does. Psychics read the energy field around your body. They read your vibration. They can tell by reading your thoughts at that precise moment, what your destiny will be. The moment you leave their presence, though, you have the ability to change your thoughts and, consequently, change the outcome. At this particular time in my life, however, I had not yet learned the lesson of going within. So this psychic, who was also a Reiki Master, read the energy around my thoughts and she told me which road I would be most likely to take. The moment she uttered the words, I was so relieved and said emphatically to her, "Oh good, that's what I **wanted** to do".

"That's what I **wanted** to do?" All along, I had been saying, "What **should** I do?" when the answer lay within the question, "What do I **want**?" This is vital to know in developing Intuition. Intuition means knowing what you want, not what you should do. The answer is right within you, always. Ask yourself. You will know what you want by how you feel. This incident proved to be the last time I would ask outside of myself for answers to any major life question.

Whenever you are in the midst of making an important decision, visualize one way you can go. Picture yourself going down that road. How does it feel? Now picture yourself going down the other road. How does it feel? This is how you get in touch with what you want. It is a powerful way to strengthen your Intuition.

PRE-PAVE in Creating

I ask myself today, "How do I feel?" "What do I want?"

PRE-PAVE: *I ask myself today, "How do I feel?" "What do I want?"*

Repeat these questions to yourself continuously throughout the day. It is very important. You need to be aware of your feelings so that you know if you are on track or not; that is, if you are **creating** what you want. If you have a negative feeling, it means you need to change your thought. Identify your feelings quickly in order to change your thought before the negative feeling manifests into the physical realm. The moment you feel different, ask yourself, "How do I feel?" If it is a good feeling, celebrate and know you are on the right track. Keep thinking positive thoughts. They are taking you in the direction you want. Take this opportunity to strengthen them.

On the other hand, if you tune in to your feelings and you find negativity (anger, fear or sadness) this is also a sign. Acknowledge what you are feeling, then ask yourself, "What do I want?" Now move your thoughts into alignment by pre-paving what you want. Your desires will manifest according to the amount of power you inject into your thoughts and to the degree of conviction and belief you put into them.

PRE-PAVE in Creating

I cultivate desires that are in
tune with my higher purpose.

PRE-PAVE: *I cultivate desires that are in tune with my higher purpose.*

When you are in a state of desire, you will naturally hope these desires are in tune with your higher purpose. Reality is, they may not be. It is very important to ensure your desires are in line with what is best for your Soul. You are only setting yourself up for unhappiness if you chase after desires that will disappoint you in the end.

So then, how to cultivate desires that are in tune with your Higher Self? You will know at the deepest level. If you ache for something with attachment, this is an indication that something is out of alignment. It doesn't mean it's not good for you, it just means that you are not in the proper state of desire. Any negative feeling surrounding a desire indicates the same thing.

When your desire is in tune with your Higher Self, you will know. You will feel it on all levels. Here are a few basic questions you can ask yourself:

• Will manifestation of my desire bring me long-term happiness?

• Will it serve others?

• Will it make me a better person?

• Will it make the world a better place?

• When I picture myself with this desire manifested, how does it make me feel?

Sincerely ask yourself these questions and you will know whether your desires are in line with your true purpose in life.

PRE-PAVE in Creating

Today I spend time writing
about what I want.

PRE-PAVE: *Today I spend time writing about what I want.*

I highly recommend the technique of journaling for gaining clarity. Not just any ordinary journaling. I teach a method of journaling called *The Journal of Positive Intentions.* Purchase a journal, or create one yourself using lined paper. It should be pleasing to the eye so that you look forward to writing in it. Before you write, make sure you are in a good mood. If listening to a certain song gets you there, do that. If playing with your dog gets you in that great frame of mind, then do that. Do whatever it takes to make sure that when you write, you are writing in a positive mental state.

Sit down to write and focus on no more than three areas of your life at a time. You could focus on relationships, work and a personal goal if you wish. Then write. Write what is in your heart. The key is to write only in the positive. You do not write anything negative in this journal. There is no such thing as exclusion in the Law of Attraction. Whatever you write about, you attract. So write about all of the things that you want. Put your whole feeling into it. Dream big with no limits.

I have over twenty of these journals from the past ten years. As I go through and review what I have written, I discover that everything I have written I have achieved in some way or another. One journal I reviewed recently described the car I drive today, the model and color in detail. I had even forgotten this was the car I wanted, until I re-read my journals from several years ago. My entire business I created through these journals, from the ground up.

If you feel unclear about what you want, start yourself a Positive Intentions Journal. Believe me, it helps you discover what it is that you want out of life. Once your pen starts writing, you will be amazed at what shows up on the page.

Remember to write only in the positive. Always start your journaling in a positive state of mind. When you write, put your whole feeling into it, and dream big. This technique works.

PRE-PAVE in Creating

I spend time today
dreaming big.

PRE-PAVE: *I spend time today dreaming big.*

If you want to play the piano and you practice thirty minutes a day, in one month you would see a significant difference in your abilities. Imagine after a year of practice.

If you want to create something, isn't it worth spending thirty minutes a day creating, just creating? Spend time thinking about what you want in your life. Focusing on it and visualizing it is time well spent. If you make this a daily habit, how much do you think this would affect your ability to create whatever you want in your life?

Carve out some time in the day to do nothing else but create. It is so powerful!

PRE-PAVE in Creating

I focus on my goals.

PRE-PAVE: *I focus on my goals.*

No matter what life throws at you in a day, always keep focused on your goals. You may have many goals in different areas of your life, so whatever you happen to be involved in at the time, focus on your goal in that area. If something that looks like it should happen to come in your way as a challenge, ask yourself, "Does it matter to my goal?" If not, then cross it off. It's not a challenge. And put your focus back on your goal again.

I have been in the process of moving my life direction from spa owner to international speaker and author recently. I have been speaking and teaching now for several years, but always as a side interest while my main interest was to grow my company, RnR Wellness. In light of my evolving career, I have been grooming people to take my place in the day-to-day operation of RnR Wellness, to free up my time for traveling and teaching full-time. You can imagine the work-load of having two feet in different boats while trying to focus full-time in each boat during the transition. It is when our agendas are this full that we truly learn to delegate the non-essentials. An issue came up at the spa recently that normally would have required my full attention. I reminded myself that my focus now was speaking and writing, so I happily delegated the matter to my Spa Director. She was more than able to handle the situation; far better than me, I might add. I mentally dropped the scenario from my mind, pre-paving it would be dealt with effectively. I continued to focus on my goal, because that was what I was creating. This is what I mean by focusing on your goals and mentally dropping all lesser things.

> *Don't sweat the small stuff.*
> *– Richard Carlson*

PRE-PAVE in Creating

I will persevere.

PRE-PAVE: *I will persevere.*

If you plug in a tea kettle for twenty seconds, then unplug it for a few minutes, and you keep repeating this process, you will never boil water. So it is with conscious creating. It is called the Tea Kettle Theory. When you want to create something, you need to hold onto a positive thought pattern in order to create it. That is what perseverance is all about.

The most common complaint from people who are just learning to use the Law of Attraction is what to do when things don't go quite as planned. This is very important to learn about, because you can bet this will happen. You have past tendencies and karma that play a role. Sometimes, it will seem as though your plan isn't working, but in essence, it is. That is why perseverance is key. Keep focusing on your goal and it will manifest. Pre-pave daily, "I will persevere", especially when things don't go your way. It is only a test. Stay focused on your plan, keeping a sustained pattern of thought in the direction you want to go. Like the tea kettle, plug yourself in to that thought pattern until you see your idea through.

PRE-PAVE in Creating

I know I can do this.

PRE-PAVE: *I know I can do this.*

After desire, belief is the next step in creating. With this pre-pave, you create belief in yourself that whatever you are attempting to do, you can do. Your conscious mind tells the sub-conscious mind that this is true. Your sub-conscious mind cannot decipher between reality and a wish. So it makes it come true!

> *Whether you believe you can do a thing*
> *or not, you are right.*
>
> *– Henry Ford*

PRE-PAVE in Creating

I expect the best and I
believe in the best.

PRE-PAVE: *I expect the best and I believe in the best.*

I'll see it when I believe it.

Your expectations become your intentions and what you intend you create. If you go through life expecting that you will be served the best food, receive the best service and be treated in the kindest way, that is what you will get.

From a young age, I have always been treated gently by others. I don't know how to describe it other than it was just my reality. So I came to expect it. I still expect it in my life. I find that, even when someone is trying to deliver bad news, they do as Burton Cummings sings about; they *break it to me gently*. Since it has been my experience, I expect it. Expecting it has fueled my belief and my belief has created my reality. When we experience life in a certain way, we come to expect it to continue. This can work for us or against us. The key is to have it work for you.

Expect the best always. Despite what you might have received previously, expect the very best this time. I said this recently in one of my classes and a student immediately responded that her motto was this: "I'll believe it when I see it." I suggested she shift her motto to the opposite, "I'll see it when I believe it". Believe it first. Then you will see it.

Some things have to be believed to be seen.

– Ralph Hodgson

PRE-PAVE in Creating

I associate with people
who support my goals.

PRE-PAVE: *I associate with people who support my goals.*

The Masters of India counsel very strongly in this area. No matter how hard you may try to reach your goals, if you surround yourself with people that go against who you want to be, you will come against temptation and distraction that will lead you away from your destination.

> *Company is stronger than will.*
>
> *– Paramahansa Yogananda*

If you slice an onion, you cannot help but have the lingering smell of onion on your hands. Everything has a vibration. If you choose to listen to music that has profanity and harsh melodies, you are bringing that vibration into your own consciousness. It cannot help but affect you in a negative way. If the video you rent on a Friday night is filled with violence, your whole vibration will change as you watch the film and experience the emotions of the characters. The people you choose to associate with are the same. Their tendencies will become your tendencies. Their standards will become your standards. Their lifestyle will become your lifestyle. It is energy and vibration. If you want to be an artist, mix with artists. If you want to be a saint, mix with saints.

> *When the character of a man is not clear to you, look at his friends.*
>
> *– Japanese Proverb*

PRE-PAVE in Creating

I follow through on my
resolutions.

PRE-PAVE: *I follow through on my resolutions.*

It is great to be inspired for the moment as we watch an inspirational film, or read an uplifting book. As we write our New Year's resolutions, we are also in a moment of inspiration, ready to take on the world! But the one thing important here is follow-through.

Often people get overwhelmed by making too many promises. In the end they keep none. I liken this to when I go on an annual Meditation Conference every summer in California. It is an amazing week of classes, workshops and meditations led by enlightened monks and nuns of Paramahansa Yogananda's organization. This annual week is chock full of wisdom. I always feel like my cup runneth over. I take intensive notes in every class. I listen with my whole heart. I capture every morsel of wisdom so I can then go back into my daily life and implement it. But to implement it all at once would be overwhelming. So I review my notes every night and I highlight the most poignant concepts. I re-read my entire journal on the airplane trip home. Before I land on home soil, I make a conscious decision to embrace two or three new habits as my own. These things I promise to incorporate into my life. I pre-pave that I will follow-through, and I do.

An idea that is developed and put into action is more important than an idea that exists only as an idea.

— Buddha

PRE-PAVE in Creating

I believe in miracles.

PRE-PAVE: *I believe in miracles.*

People often question how the Universe will provide them with something. They put out a desire, then wonder how on Earth it could be made manifest, especially if they deem the desire as too huge or unattainable for them. Know for certain, that when you doubt or question, you send a message to the Universe to cancel out your creation. This also puts your desire in a state of resistance.

Do not look for the "how". Leave that to the Divine. It is what "miracles" are reserved for. Plenty of miracles go on within the Laws in order to fulfill your desires. How else do you think it would be possible? Believe in miracles.

PAVING IT FORWARD
in Giving

PAVING IT FORWARD – IN GIVING

We make a living by what we get.
We make a life by what we give.

– Sir Winston Churchill

PRE-PAVE in Giving

Whatever I need, I focus
on giving it.

PRE-PAVE: *Whatever I need, I focus on giving it.*

Whatever you want, you can have, but you must learn how to give it first. In other words, that which you give, you receive. It is called the Law of Giving. If you want to be respected, you must resonate respect. You resonate respect by putting thoughts of respect into your energy field, which is your vibration. You do this by respecting yourself and by respecting others. If you fill your vibration with thoughts of feeling resentful that people are not respecting you, you will not attract respect.

The Law of Giving: That which you give, you receive.

If you want love, you must resonate love. Your vibration must be filled with thoughts of love. It does not matter what form of love you give, as long as you are filling your energy field with love. You can focus on loving yourself, loving a parent or loving a child. In return, the Universe will bring love to you, in whatever form your Soul craves the most.

You alone must fill your heart, mind and Soul with the qualities you want to experience. The moment you resonate these qualities, you begin to attract them immediately. It is Universal Law.

You must give some time to your fellow men. Even if it's a little thing, do something for others – something for which you get no pay but the privilege of doing it.

– Albert Schweitzer

PRE-PAVE in Giving

I give for the joy of giving.

PRE-PAVE: *I give for the joy of giving.*

The Law of Giving is always at work. When you truly understand the energy behind giving, it will guide you to give in the right spirit. The spirit in which you give to others is the most important thing in the process of giving. In fact, it is everything. It has a tremendous effect on what you attract in return.

If you give with an expectation of return, you resonate "expectation". Believe me, this is more common than you might think. Become aware of your motives as you are giving. Giving selflessly without conditions attached raises your vibration. In turn, what you give comes back to you tenfold.

There is a common misconception that you receive from the source to which you give. Often, this is not so. I coach a lot of people in this area. If you feel frustrated or resentful after continuously giving to a certain person without receiving anything in return, I say to you, keep on giving. You have no idea where and how it will return to you, but know for certain, it will return. When you question or doubt, you put negative thoughts into your vibrational field sending a message to the Universe to cancel out your creation.

The Kabbalah* teaches of the rewards of donating anonymously. To give without desire of recognition is to truly give. When you focus on giving, for the joy of it alone, you resonate **service**. When you give in the right spirit, Universal Law will bring it back to you without fail. The Law of Giving is always at work.

Now, there will be times when you know in your heart that a situation is going nowhere. You are giving in a certain area and you feel that your efforts would be much more beneficial and appreciated if you gave in another area. It is perfectly fine for you

---

*KABBALAH DEFINITION: TRADITION WITHIN JUDAISM WHICH FOCUSES ON MYSTICAL INTERPRETATIONS OF SCRIPTURE AND ESOTERIC DOCTRINES ABOUT THE BEING OF GOD

to retreat from giving in that direction, as long as you acknowledge it in a positive way. If you make a conscious choice to give here instead of there, with positive thoughts and with no thought of return, you can change your direction of giving at any time. Do you see the difference?

Have you ever opened a Christmas gift and found that the gift was more expensive or more thoughtful than the one you gave this person and you immediately felt bad about it? First of all, feeling bad about anything puts the wrong mind chemistry into your vibration, so change the thought right way. Accept the beautiful gift. Be grateful. Do not compare it. When you are giving gifts to people, do not give according to what you anticipate they will give you. Give from your heart, something you think will change their world, without any thought of comparing it to what they might be giving you.

I was recently discussing Christmas with my family. My two older children, pre-teen age, were sharing their thoughts on whether Santa Claus physically existed or not. Our son explained it so eloquently to his little sister that "Santa Claus represents the spirit of giving. In essence, Santa Claus is real." How true that is.

How often are we running about in December trying to scratch everyone off the list instead of spending December in a spirit of giving?

The spirit in which a thing is given determines that in which the debt is acknowledged; it is the intention, not the face value of the gift, that is weighed.

— Seneca

PRE-PAVE in Giving

I give my greatest gift, myself.

PRE-PAVE: *I give my greatest gift, myself.*

We can spoil children with toys, but the best gift we can give them is the gift of our time. What our loved ones want most from us is our attention. Being present with a child for one hour has much more impact than coming home with the latest and greatest video game. Most of us have no idea how much the people close to us crave our attention.

Too much time in front of the television takes away from personal interaction. In most cases, it boils down to a number of people watching a square flat tube mounted to the wall, but not connecting with each other. Try not watching TV for a whole day and replace that time with sincerely connecting with your family and friends.

Be present with people today. A great time to connect is over dinner. Look into each other's eyes, not just at the food. Be present as you are sitting beside each other in the car. Take your partner's hand and give it a gentle squeeze that says "I love you, I'm here for you." Being present is the greatest gift you can give to others. The people around you need you. When you come home with the intention of giving yourself to your family, a great awareness will come over you. You will see them in a different light. You will wake up to what you have been missing for perhaps a very long time.

> *What a child doesn't receive,*
> *he can seldom later give.*
>
> *– P. D. James*

PAVING IT FORWARD
in Travel

PAVING IT FORWARD – IN TRAVEL

These pre-paves are to help you in any type of travel, both work and pleasure, including that much-anticipated vacation time. Vacations are an important time to pre-pave what you want. They are a time of refuge, an escape from your day-to-day life. With travel, unfortunately, we often experience time delays, luggage issues or cancelled flights that can spell stress or disappointment. When this happens, things can spiral from bad to worse. We've all said at one point, "It's good to go away, but it's always great to come home". Pre-paving can drastically help make your daily commute or your vacation travel experience enjoyable and safe.

For many years, I traveled for a living. I was on four to five flights a week. People used to ask me if I ever got tired of the airports and commuting. I absolutely loved the thrill of it. I pre-paved what I wanted to experience and I enjoyed my work commutes as mini-vacations. I would use the time to get caught up on paperwork on the airplane. If things were under control, I would treat myself to a new book to relax. Regardless, it was **me** time with no demands. I pre-paved it always to be a positive experience.

PRE-PAVE in Travel

I pre-pave safety. I am safe.

PRE-PAVE: *I pre-pave safety. I am safe.*

This pre-pave is something you really should practice every time you get behind the wheel, or any time you get in the passenger side or back seat for that matter. Pre-paving safety prior to boarding an airplane, train or boat, wherever you are headed, lines up the energy to keep you safe.*

If you pre-pave safety as you are making your flight reservations, the Universe will guide you to choosing the correct flight to get you to your destination safely. Do not question and do not underestimate the power of energy and how it works to guide you toward what you have pre-paved.

---

*MORE INFORMATION IN THE INTRODUCTORY CHAPTERS ON
PRE-PAVING SAFETY.

PRE-PAVE in Travel

My car is reliable.
I can always depend on it.

PRE-PAVE: *My car is reliable. I can always depend on it.*

M ost people have no idea the effect their thoughts have on inanimate objects. Everything has a vibration. The objects you own and use take on your vibration, and they respond according to your thoughts and expectations of them.

When I studied Reiki from Elizabeth Gilberg, she used to tell us stories about how she could use Reiki to fix her kitchen appliances. Her toaster was determined to fail, but she kept fixing it with Reiki energy every time she wanted to use it. It was no fluke. It was real. I, too, have practiced this and it works.

Inanimate objects work in accordance with our demand thoughts.

Inanimate objects are at the command of your thought. When you study Reiki, you learn how to send light to your car and other objects that you rely on to operate safely. You do not need to know Reiki in order to do this. Just visualize the object surrounded in light and intend that it be done. A thought has a frequency just like a radio wave has a frequency. Everything is made of the same mind-stuff. There is no difference between the radio and the car battery. The power of your thought can heal yourself, a friend and even your car. We are all made of the same substance.

PRE-PAVE in Travel

I reach my destination quickly
and efficiently.

PRE-PAVE: *I reach my destination quickly and efficiently.*

Often, people pre-pave "traffic". Yes, that is right; they get into their cars and say to themselves, "Gee, I hope the traffic isn't bad today." Without realizing it, they are vibrating and pre-paving "traffic". Remember, there is no such thing as exclusion in the Law of Attraction. What you think about, talk about and write about, you attract.

Next time you are about to enter into rush-hour traffic, change your thought and practice the positive pre-pave above instead. Pre-pave that the roads will be surprisingly clear and cars moving quickly. Predict that street-lights will be timed perfectly to let you through. Watch how the road clears up ahead of you. The Universe will guide you to the route that is clear. Listen to your Intuition as you drive.

PRE-PAVE in Travel

I choose the perfect place for my trip.

PRE-PAVE: *I choose the perfect place for my trip.*

Have you ever chosen the wrong venue for your vacation, the wrong tour, the wrong restaurant or the wrong hotel? At one point or another in our lives, most of us have been on a vacation that didn't match up to our dreams. Vacation time is so important. It is your re-creation time; a time to relax or play or just get away from the "busy-ness" of life. You have earned it and you want it to be everything you dreamed it would be.

If you end up having a bad experience, the tendency is to start planning your next vacation with an adamant intention that you won't let it happen again. These thoughts actually re-create the experience. You are simply pre-paving another unfavorable situation. For example, if you say to yourself, "Oh I hope this hotel is better than the last one we were at; wasn't it terrible?", you bring the feeling of your last experience into your current vibration. With these words and thoughts, you are pre-paving a similar experience. The Universe brings you what you feel and what you focus on.

Instead, pre-pave that you will choose the perfect place. Feel how you want to feel as you arrive. Visualize what you want to see. Pre-pave what weather you want to have! Why not? You are creating your experience with your thoughts. Choose it now, rather than being a victim of circumstance. Visualize everything that you want, to the last detail. Then hear yourself say *"I love it!"* and it will be so.

It is better to travel well, than to arrive.

– Buddha

PRE-PAVE in Travel

I am going to have a great time.

PRE-PAVE: *I am going to have a great time.*

I love open-ended general pre-paves that deal with how you feel because they are the most powerful. When I go out for an evening or go on vacation, I may not necessarily know exactly how everything should look, but I certainly know how I want to feel. I want to feel great. I want to have a great time. That is all you need to know sometimes when you pre-pave a good experience.

Who doesn't remember the movie *Pretty Woman* – the scene where Julia Roberts is just about to be whisked away by Richard Gere in a helicopter for a romantic dinner; every girl's dream date. They are dressed to the nines and as they're ready to leave the hotel, she stops him before the evening begins. She has no idea what he has in store for her, but she says to him, "If I forget to tell you later, I had a great time tonight." It was a classic scene, and the perfect pre-pave for a perfect evening.

Pre-pave always that you will have a great time, whether it's a week's vacation or an evening out with a loved one. Your feelings are created by your thoughts. Create what you want to feel before the experience by pre-paving it.

PAVING IT FORWARD
in Health

There are seven major energy centers in the body, from the base of the spine up to the crown of the head. If you could see them, you would see funnels of energy projecting out of the top, bottom, front, and back of the body. To be in perfect health, energy must flow freely through these energy centers without obstruction.

Every thought you think enters your energy field immediately. When you think a negative thought, it puts a little dark cloud into your vibration. When you sustain that thought, or add other negative thoughts to it, the dark cloud gets larger and starts to block the flow of energy around your body. It works like a snowball effect.

When the block gets large enough to completely stop the flow of energy, it then enters the body. It has nowhere else to go. In essence, negative thoughts start in the energy field, then manifest in the body in the form of ill-health. This could mean a mild headache, an ulcer or even something as serious as cancer. Studies have been conducted proposing a link between cancer and feelings of anger. If you hold sustained thoughts of anger in your mind, imagine what that does to your energy field. This field is your vibration, your magnet that attracts to you everything you have in your life, including your state of health.

On a positive note, there are ways to instantly raise your vibration toward health. The moment you smile a sincere smile, your entire vibration lights up, becomes brighter and expands. This is also true when you are in a state of appreciation, when you are expressing true love for another, when you are praying for someone, or when you are focusing on healing yourself or others. Any positive emotion will brighten your energy field and immediately start to attract good health to you. You are a powerful being. You can make yourself ill or well, right within the realm of your inner thought.

PRE-PAVE in Health

I pre-pave good health.

PRE-PAVE: *I pre-pave good health.*

Have you asked for health? With our choice of thoughts and words, we end up in a certain state of health because we have unconsciously asked for it. Ask and you shall receive. Your vibration is **always** asking, and the Universe is **always** providing. You ask with your vibration. Wake up in the morning and pre-pave good health. Tell the Universe how you want to feel and what kind of health you want.

Ask and you shall receive.

— Jesus Christ

PRE-PAVE in Health

I think, speak and act of health.

PRE-PAVE: *I think, speak and act of health.*

Regardless of how you feel, if you want to change your health for the better, you must start thinking, speaking and acting as though you were already healthy now. I have heard people speak of a recent surgery. When I comment on how quickly they have recovered, they share with me, "Oh it was over twenty years ago". They speak of it as though it were just yesterday. We can make ourselves ill by re-hashing past ill experiences. We can make ourselves well by choosing to release past pains and move forward toward good health.

If you find yourself with a headache, this is the perfect time to pre-pave good health. The tendency for people is to tell others they have a headache, which tells the Universe to keep the pain coming. I know it is tempting to talk about it. It is natural to look for sympathy. But what could be more tempting than feeling good instead? The moment you get even the slightest indication of ill-health, focus your thoughts and words on a pre-pave toward wellness. Believe it and it will come true.

If you do this and an hour later the pain persists, do not succumb to the temptation of talking about how you tried to change it with your mind but it didn't work. If you do this, you are giving the Universe another signal to keep it coming. You get the picture. Despite any pain you might be feeling, keep paving forward good health and it must manifest. It is Universal Law.

> *Every human being is the author of his own health or disease.*
>
> *— Buddha*

PRE-PAVE in Health

I replace my bodily cells daily
with new healthy cells.

PRE-PAVE: *I replace my bodily cells daily with new healthy cells.*

C ells in your body are constantly regenerating themselves. The **you** that is sitting here does not have even one cell the same as the **you** that would have sat here seven years ago. Does it not stand to reason then, that we can heal ourselves by creating new, healthy cells every day where there might have been cells of ill-health before? This is much of the focus of Deepak Chopra's teachings.

We get what we focus on. What would happen if you spent a few moments every day, completely focused on replacing your body with healthy cells, by intending it with your thoughts? How do you think this would affect your state of health? In my audio CD called *Transformation** there is a wonderful healing exercise called the Rainshower Meditation. I urge you to practice it. It uses a Reiki technique of totally cleansing the body's cells, washing away any negative dark clouds in your vibration and replacing each cell with a healing vibration.

PRE-PAVE in Health

I fill my body with Light.

PRE-PAVE: *I fill my body with Light.*

Reiki is an ancient Japanese form of energy healing that has been termed the "laying on of hands". A traditional Reiki session is performed on a massage bed. The practitioner places his or her hands on the various energy centers of the body, usually focusing on the seven main centers, but spending the majority of time intuitively on the area that needs the most healing. Most Reiki Masters can either see or feel energy. I am a Reiki Master, which is the driving force behind the focus of **energy** in my talks and writings.

Every thought you think hovers in your energy field. A Reiki session can be likened to receiving a "bath of light". Imagine what that would do in cleaning up your vibration and helping you to attract good things. Reiki Masters can sense and remove large blocks of energy from the body or energy field surrounding the body. When they are removed, you feel incredible.

I like to teach that we are all healers, not just those who study or practice a formal method of healing. You have healing power in your hands. If you have a stomach ache, place your hands on your stomach with the intent of healing yourself. You will be able to feel heat emanating from your hands. This is healing energy. It fills your stomach with light. You can use this method to heal any part of your body as well as ailments of the mind such as a feeling of being overwhelmed, or a broken heart. Intuitively ask yourself what area of the body is represented by your pain. The first answer that comes to mind is the correct answer. It could be your head, your heart, your throat or wherever you are guided. Place your hands on that spot and intend that you are sending light there.

Why does a mother instantly place her hand on her child where it hurts? Children will intuitively grab the hand of the mother and place it on their painful spot. You can heal yourself by sending healing light through your hands to the afflicted part. For an overall healing of the body, you can intend for your entire body to be filled with light. You will be able to feel the light entering your body. It feels like a warm, soothing wave, or sometimes a tingling feeling, or even coolness. Everyone will experience something unique but similar, and you will definitely be able to feel it if you practice sincerely.

I never go to sleep at night without filling my entire body with light by placing both hands on my head. I feel the wave of energy enter my body and visualize the light cleanse me from head to toe. You do not need to be a Reiki Master to do this. All you need is a desire to be healed and intend that you have the power to heal yourself.

PRE-PAVE in Health

I pray for the healing of others.

PRE-PAVE: *I pray for the healing of others.*

The Masters of India teach that one cannot reach Enlightenment without including and helping others along the way. It means caring for others as you care for yourself. Praying for others is integral to your own health, happiness and success. Your thoughts are so powerful. If you spend time every day sending healing light to others, you will change their lives and your own.

It is important to know how to pray effectively. Perhaps you have a friend suffering from cancer and each night you pray that he or she be free of cancer. If you picture this person suffering in a hospital bed, you are not praying effectively. You are filling your vibration with negative thoughts. This is really important to know. The Universe works on Law. It will bring you what you focus on. Even though you may think you are doing a good deed, when you focus on the cancer, you are actually attracting ill-health to yourself and you are truly not helping your friend.

The most effective way to heal others is to visualize them surrounded in light. This also surrounds you in light. Imagine what you can do for yourself and others by practicing this every day. Visualize their body immersed in light; the light penetrating every cell with a healing vibration. Visualize them happy, healthy and whole. Picture them as you know they would like to be. This is, by far, the most powerful thing you can do to help a friend in need. It is more than anything physical you could do for them. As you help others, your own vibration is raised, purified and healed.

PAVING IT FORWARD
in Wealth

PAVING IT FORWARD – IN WEALTH

Do not confuse wealth with financial status. Wealth is a state of abundance, which includes family, health, happiness, love and yes, money. If you want to attract financial wealth in particular, begin by feeling wealthy with all of the other things that mean abundance. Then you will vibrate wealth, and the Universe will bring to you the financial wealth you seek.

PRE-PAVE in Wealth

I appreciate my house, my
electricity, my telephone,
my car.

PRE-PAVE: *I appreciate my house, my electricity, my telephone, my car.*

We enjoy our belongings, but often the things we pay for on a monthly basis can cause us grief as the bills arrive on our doorstep. Let me give you a tip: pay your bills with gratitude. Smile as you are writing the cheques. Be appreciative of the service or products you received. Think how grateful you are for the enjoyment of these things. Be happy knowing that you will always have the money to pay your bills. The energy you emit with this attitude will create great wealth for you. Try it. It truly works.

PRE-PAVE in Wealth

All of my needs are met,
now and always.

PRE-PAVE: *All of my needs are met, now and always.*

This is about trust. Yes, we plan for the future, but we live today, trusting that our needs in the future will always be met. This consciousness felt and understood at a deep level, will create for you exactly what you need. You cannot doubt. If you wonder how the Universe will manifest it, you cancel out your creation. Trust, believe and pave it forward.

The affirmation below is very powerful in transforming your mind toward wealth consciousness. Practice it over and over again with your pre-pave and it will change the cells in your brain for creating wealth.

> *I go forth in perfect faith in the power of*
> *Omnipresent Good,*
> *to bring me what I need, at the time I need it.*
>
> *– Paramahansa Yogananda*

PRE-PAVE in Wealth

I need $____ to do
or to buy_____.

PRE-PAVE: *I need $____ to do or to buy _____.*

In my classes, students have shared with me numerous stories of incredible manifestation.

One lady told me a story about how she had asked the Universe for $110,000.00. She needed it for a specific purpose. This was the amount she wanted and she asked for it with conviction. She truly believed that she deserved to receive it. Within six months, she received an inheritance from a wealthy uncle who passed away in the United States. It was for an exact amount of U.S. funds that converted to $110,000.00 in Canadian dollars.

There is nothing too large or too small to the Universe. The Universe can manifest ten dollars just the same as it can manifest ten thousand. It is your belief that determines what is large or small, difficult or easy. Your mind is what puts limits on what the Universe will manifest for you. Pre-pave what you need, for whatever you need it, and believe in your power.

PRE-PAVE in Wealth

Every day I feel more and
more wealthy.

PRE-PAVE: *Every day I feel more and more wealthy.*

A man was having trouble with his finances and so he went for counseling. After an hour-long session, he eagerly left the office feeling very confident with his new-found techniques on how to create wealth in his life. Two weeks later he arrived back at the office for his next session, moping and miserable. When the counselor asked him about his obvious distress, the man responded, "Counselor, my financial situation has spiraled for the worse. I did what you said. I affirmed morning, noon and night, *I am wealthy, I am wealthy, I am wealthy...*I knew it wasn't going to work!"

Whatever you pave forward, you must believe. That is why pre-paving how you will feel about wealth is wise, because what you feel is what you will believe and what you believe is what you will create.

PRE-PAVE in Wealth

I keep focused on my
financial success.

PRE-PAVE: *I keep focused on my financial success.*

Do not anticipate trouble, or worry about what may never happen. Keep in the sunlight.

There was a successful hot dog vendor named Francis who lived and operated his little business in New York City. Every day there were long line-ups of people at his hot dog stand. He served the most delicious hot dogs in the city. People traveled several city blocks just to indulge in these tasty treats. One day, the vendor's son came up to his father and exclaimed with passion, "Father! Father! Have you not read the papers? There is a depression in the city of New York! Half of the shops on our street are closing down!" In anticipation of the effects of the depression, Francis packed up his vending station and closed up shop.

Another true story is about a friend of mine, Paul Ramikie, who has been a successful realtor in Calgary for over thirty years. In the early 1980's, there was a downturn in the Calgary economy. Many businesses who had ridden the wave of the boom were now feeling the harsh effects of the fall. Of course, it was the hot topic of discussion in the media and among Calgarians. Despite the city's decline, Paul still seemed to maintain his normal share of the marketplace and was enjoying the financial rewards that his colleagues were not. At a company function, a man from the company approached Paul's wife, Gemma, and introduced himself to her. Once he found out who she was, he exclaimed, "Oh, you're married to the guy who doesn't know we're in a recession!"

You will only be affected by the ups and downs of the world if you identify yourself with them. The Universe is abundant. It can create anything for you, despite any outward economic fluctuations. Hold fast to your goals of financial success, regardless of what others and the world are doing around you.

Energy and persistence conquer all things.

– Benjamin Franklin

PAVING IT FORWARD
in Adversity

Adversity sparks us to make a change. It gives us an opportunity to release old patterns that may not be serving us well. Tests and trials are a wake-up call. When received in the right spirit, they can be the greatest blessing of our lives.

Successfully dealing with adversity really boils down to one thing: *Right Attitude*. Great characters are built during tests and trials, especially when approached in the right frame of mind. Adversity is your teacher, your friend. Smile. Face it and be grateful for the experience.

Life is a reflection back to you of your own state of consciousness. When you change your way of thinking, everything on the outside changes. In knowing that, you can move what might seem to be a challenge, into what you could call a gift.

We don't see things as they are,
we see things as we are.

– Anais Nin

PRE-PAVE in Adversity

Change no circumstance in
my life. Change me.

PRE-PAVE: *Change no circumstance in my life. Change me.*

Written by a saint of the twentieth century, Sister Gyanamata, this pre-pave is loaded with dynamite. I suggest you recite it many times throughout the day as a prayer or mantra. Say it as often as you can, with deep concentration. If you are in dire need of changing everything around you, this pre-pave will move mountains.

How often have you said, "When this happens, then I will be happy" or, "When I have this or that, then I can be at peace". We often want things outside of us to change, but we don't realize that it is something within us that must change first. It is a myth that you cannot change others and circumstances. You most certainly can, but only by changing yourself will you have the experience.

Practice this pre-pave whenever things get tough. Practice it with sincerity and conviction, and you will come to understand its power. You cannot describe how an orange tastes; you must taste it for yourself. I urge you to taste this orange for yourself.

In looking for externals to change, we often fail to see what inside of us needs to change. When you use this pre-pave, whatever is inside of you that needs changing will become known to you. It opens your eyes to a greater understanding of everything around you.

You must be the change you wish to see in the world.
— Mahatma Gandhi

PRE-PAVE in Adversity

Today I change one thing
about myself.

PRE-PAVE: *Today I change one thing about myself.*

This pre-pave is a conviction that you will follow through with the change that you feel is the most important at this time. There is nothing easy or difficult in the realm of the Universe. Something you might have deemed as difficult to change is no different in the eyes of the Universe than something you might think is easy. This is one explanation for how addictions can be overcome. A pattern of behavior is only difficult to change if you deem it to be so.

Set your intention of making the change that you want. If you say this pre-pave without knowing what it is you want to change, then intend that the change be made, regardless of your conscious awareness of it.

There is nothing like returning to a place that remains unchanged, to find the ways in which you yourself have altered.

– Nelson Mandela

PRE-PAVE in Adversity

My environment is perfect
for me.

PRE-PAVE: *My environment is perfect for me.*

If you could but see the big picture of life, you would realize that your current environment is truly perfect for what your Soul needs right at this moment in time. As much as you might think you are dealing with an adverse situation, when you look to the higher purpose of what is transpiring, you can rise above the challenge. Allow it to take its course, accepting it as perfect in the moment.

> *Insanity is doing the same thing over and over again expecting a different result.*

Any challenge that is not received in the right attitude will need to be re-played in the drama of life until you "get it". Adversity is brought to you to ignite a change in the way you do things. Einstein defined insanity as doing the same thing over and over again, expecting a different result. If you find yourself in the same type of challenge repeatedly, albeit different faces and places, it's time to look at changing your pattern of thought, speech or action. Your current way of doing things is not working.

PRE-PAVE in Adversity

This world is a dream.

PRE-PAVE: *This world is a dream.*

I t feels good to pre-pave this and believe it. Feeling good; isn't that a great start? What you feel you attract. The best way to rise above life's challenges is to acknowledge that this world is a dream. It truly is. This pre-pave gets me out of a slump every single time without fail.

Life is a drama and you are the star actor creating your own play under the Master Director. When you rise above and know that you are just playing a part in the Master Novel of the Universe, you can take things more lightly and remove yourself from the experience. Only when you become attached to the drama, do you put yourself in a position where you can get hurt.

A good novel or drama needs a villain and a hero. It is only interesting if it has twists and turns, tragedy and comic relief. If this worldly drama consisted of angels morning, noon and night, everyone would be walking around yawning of boredom. Life is so enticing because of its drama. When you read a novel, sometimes the chapters seem confusing with many different characters and sub-plots. But at the end, everything makes sense. Everything is tied together and then you understand the meaning of it all. Trust that everything in this grand scheme of life does make sense, and will make sense to you, when the time is right. The right time can be now, when you rise above your challenges with this mental attitude.

You can go further with this pre-pave and say, "This is not my home". The Masters of India teach this. This is not your home. Your home is Omnipresence*. Your home is of another world. Do your best and be non-attached. One day you will have to leave it all for a much better place. When you are non-attached to the outcome, you can rise above any difficulty.

---

*Omnipresence: awareness of everything in Creation   *Paving it Forward - In Adversity* **255**

PRE-PAVE in Adversity

I am compassionate with
myself and others.

PRE-PAVE: *I am compassionate with myself and others.*

A dversity is often the perfect platform for learning the art of compassion. There is nothing like a humiliating failure to give you compassion for the faults of others. It is more tempting to be judgmental and critical of others when we feel we ourselves are perfect.

The other day I made a grave error. It was purely unintentional, but it could have had unspeakable effects on my life. Earlier in the day, I had been feeling a little judgmental of someone and I remembered having felt a little impatient and irritated with her weaknesses. At the end of the day, as I was experiencing my own faults and weaknesses, it opened me up to loving this person deeply. Everything happens to us to teach us something.

You don't need an experience like I had to wake you up toward compassion. Practice this pre-pave and it will help you develop a compassionate heart, without the tragedy.

PRE-PAVE in Adversity

I face my tests with courage.

PRE-PAVE: *I face my tests with courage.*

*The bravest thing you can do when you are not brave,
is to profess courage, and act accordingly.*

– Corra Harri

It is perfectly okay to feel fear. Fear guides you toward what is right and wrong. Like any negative emotion, it is a sign. It is what you do with that fear that counts. This pre-pave instills confidence within you to react to troubling circumstances with courage.

John Wayne said, "Courage is being scared to death but saddling up anyway." Everyone feels the same fear, but the courageous choose to react differently. When you pre-pave courage, you get on the saddle. The moment you take a step toward facing any challenge, you become larger than the challenge. The Masters of India teach not to pray for your troubles to be less. Rather, pray that you become larger than your troubles. Pray for the wisdom and strength to overcome them.

Courage is being scared to death but saddling up anyway.

Prayer is a form of pre-paving. Remember, the sub-conscious mind cannot distinguish between reality and a wish. When you pre-pave or pray for wisdom, courage and strength, it changes the outcome.

Face fear in the face and it will cease to trouble you.

– Swami Sri Yukteswar

PRE-PAVE in Adversity

I am becoming the person
I want to be.

PRE-PAVE: *I am becoming the person I want to be.*

What you are, is God's gift to you.
What you become, is your gift to God.

— Leo Buscaglia

Who you become is whom you choose to become. Think of someone you deeply admire. What one quality do they have that you wish you could acquire? Choose today to think, speak and act as though you already possess this quality. Make it your own. Imagine that others see it in you as you see it in yourself. Watch the Universe responding positively to you with this new quality.

It is not what happens to you that is important. It is who you become through it.

I will remind you of what I touched on earlier about energy. If you didn't already resonate that quality, you could not possibly detect it in another person. Whatever you see in another person, must to some degree or level resonate within yourself, or you could not see it. You already possess this quality that you have wished to possess. Acknowledge it now. Express it with confidence, for it is already a part of you.

PRE-PAVE in Adversity

Today I will do something I
have never done before.

PRE-PAVE: *Today I will do something I have never done before.*

I n your job, in your relationships, try this. It shakes things up and puts fresh energy into something that might have been getting mundane or going sideways. Watch how the Universe responds to you differently, to the new energy you are emitting.

> ***If you want something you've never had,***
> ***do something you've never done.***
>
> > **– Albert Einstein**

PRE-PAVE in Adversity

I release one thing today
that no longer serves me.

PRE-PAVE: *I release one thing today that no longer serves me.*

Often the challenges we face are due to holding on dearly to those things that we wish we would discard; for fear of change, perhaps? Analyze today what it is that you are holding on to for no reason. That which no longer serves you, needs to be released.

What you release today could be a habit, an emotion, an object or past commitment. You will know what it is. Ask your Intuition.

I hate to have, what I'm afraid to lose.

— William Shakespeare

PRE-PAVE in Adversity

I simplify my life.

PRE-PAVE: *I simplify my life.*

There was a fisherman who lived on a beach in Mexico. One day a businessman on vacation watched the routine of the fisherman. The fisherman would go out each day with his small boat and net and fish all morning until he caught one full net. Then he would return to the beach after taking care of his catch of the day. He would enjoy a little siesta with his family and friends until dinner-time when they would relax a little more and enjoy the sunset together.

After a few days of observing the fisherman, the businessman could not get over it. He was in awe of the opportunities this humble man was missing. Ten boats would reap ten times the fish. How could this fisherman not see this? He could rent these boats and hire the manpower to do the extra work and end up with ten times the profit at the end of the day. So the businessman approached the fisherman and eagerly pitched his idea to him. The fisherman pondered the thought, then asked the businessman, "And what would be the purpose of doing this?" The businessman responded, "So that you can make more money to enjoy afternoon siesta with your family and friends and watch the sunset together in the evenings." And to this the fisherman replied, "But I already do that", and he went back to his wife and children to continue with his siesta on the beach.

We make things so complicated when they don't need to be. Happiness is now. It is in the simple pleasures of life. Embrace and enjoy your life right now. Enjoy its beauty and simplicity.

Think of all the beauty still left around you, and be happy.
— Anne Frank

PRE-PAVE in Adversity

I react to every situation
today with calmness.

PRE-PAVE: *I react to every situation today with calmness.*

A nger is a heated state of mind that thrives when reacting to a seeming disaster. Being quick to anger was a trait of mine when I was in my early twenties, partly due to my Scorpio tendencies and being raised in an expressive family. I am grateful that a friend of mine broke me of the habit, but I can say his tactics were not as gentle as the ones I teach today.

I was twenty years old when I moved out to Alberta on my own, from Ontario. I was away from my family for the first time, so my family influence was still quite strong and a large part of my character. I experienced challenges in this new city as would be expected. Each time a situation came up that angered me, I would openly express it. My friend would not accept my behavior. He stopped me dead in my tracks. "What is this?" he would say sternly. And he would stifle my words, not allowing me to speak or express myself. Please know, I am not agreeing with this method. Quite the contrary. I teach a much softer method, as you will see further on. Nevertheless, this was my experience at this time. After repeated, painful throws to the ego, it finally clicked and I made a change.

> Anger is a heated state of mind that thrives when reacting to a seeming disaster.

Today, the method I teach to rid yourself of anger tendencies is to focus on the opposite. The opposite of anger is calmness, peace of mind. Changing your habit from anger to peace does not have to hurt when you use the technique of paving it forward. If you pre-pave calmness at the beginning of the day, the energy around every circumstance will assist you. If you prepare by saying this pre-pave before or during a typically anger-raising circumstance, the energy will come to your aid. Use it. It works. When you practice this pre-pave, you will realize that you can maintain a state of calmness through anything. The next pre-pave will help you sustain that calm state always.

Holding on to anger is like grasping a hot coal
with the intent of throwing it at someone else.
You are the one who gets burned.

— Buddha

PRE-PAVE in Adversity

I am calm, I am peaceful.

PRE-PAVE: *I am calm, I am peaceful.*

When our minds are calm, little disturbances in the day are like small pebbles causing mere ripples in the lake of our consciousness. When our minds are restless, little disturbances are like boulders causing great waves in our consciousness.

From a calm center, we make better decisions. We connect more deeply with people. We live in an awakened state of consciousness. When we are calm, we are more aware of life's constant opportunities.

> *First keep the peace within yourself,*
> *then you can also bring peace to others.*
> *— Thomas A. Kempis*

PRE-PAVE in Adversity

Today it is easy to be
patient with all people and
all circumstances.

PRE-PAVE: *Today it is easy to be patient with all people and all circumstances.*

The more we lose our patience, the more opportunities the Universe will give us to practice it. If you leave it up to the Universe to test you, it will. Instead, pre-pave that you will be patient. Patience is something you decide upon before you enter into the day. Pre-pave it in the morning, then pre-pave it throughout the day and especially just before you expect to enter into a situation that in the past has caused you to lose it.

> *We could never learn to be patient,*
> *if there were only joy in the world.*
> *— Helen Keller*

PRE-PAVE in Adversity

I allow things to be less
than perfect today.

PRE-PAVE: *I allow things to be less than perfect today.*

*The man who makes no mistakes
does not usually make anything.*
— *William Connor Magee*

Just because something isn't perfect doesn't mean it doesn't count. When we strive for perfection and fall short, we fill our vibration with guilt energy. Our vibration is our magnet and is always attracting.

Striving for perfection is sometimes associated with struggle and strain. Release the need to be perfect and drop the side-order of guilt. Yes, do your best, but enjoy where you are. Where you are right now is exactly where you need to be.

*I am careful not to confuse excellence with perfection.
Excellence I can reach for. Perfection is God's business.*
— *Michael J. Fox*

PRE-PAVE in Adversity

Today I choose to be happy.

PRE-PAVE: *Today I choose to be happy.*

Absolutely everything we have in our lives is by choice, including happiness.

A woman seventy years of age, nearly blind, was being admitted into a nursing home after having just lost her husband of fifty years. She was waiting in the lobby as a young attendant greeted her and gently helped her up from her seat by holding on to her arm. As he guided her through the hallways toward her room, he began telling her all about her room. He described it in full detail from the comfortable bed, to the top-quality matching drapes and bedspread. As he was in mid-sentence, she came to a full stop, got his attention and said, "Dear, you can stop describing it to me. I already love it. I chose to love it before I arrived."

We choose how we feel. We choose what we love.

> *No one can make you happy if you choose to be unhappy, and no one can make you unhappy if you choose to be happy.*
>
> *– Paramahansa Yogananda*

PRE-PAVE in Adversity

Today I clean up one area of
my life.

PRE-PAVE: *Today I clean up one area of my life.*

Mental clarity has a direct correlation to the degree of physical clutter we have in our lives. When we move our energy toward cleaning up the clutter from even one small area of our physical lives, a mental block is released from our creative energy.

Focus today on cleaning out one physical thing. It could be a closet, a drawer, an office or your car. Whatever it is you decide to clean today, enjoy the process. When you work with enthusiasm and willingness you receive a burst of energy to complete the job. As you purge things, feel the release of letting go of old chaos, and welcome clarity and cleanliness. Spirit can come to us only when the vessel is empty. When our physical lives become uncluttered, our mental consciousness becomes clear and receptive to new and more beautiful things.

Often, in times of adversity, we are given clarity on what we want in the process of being shown what we do not want.

PRE-PAVE in Adversity

Today I either release the
opinions of others or I learn
from them.

PRE-PAVE: *Today I either release the opinions of others or I learn from them.*

M uch of our trouble in life often stems from what we think others think of us. The opinions of others have nothing to do with you. They have everything to do with them. Look at the energy of what happens when you hold on to the opinions of others. Every thought you think enters your vibration. That includes the opinions of others, if you choose to make them your business. If you release those opinions like water off a duck's back, they have no power to affect you. Do you see how important this is?

The thoughts you choose to think, create your magnet. Hold on to only those thoughts that uplift you.

Now, there is another thought to this. If someone has said something to you and you want to learn something from it, ask yourself first with non-attachment, "Do I have that quality? Do I resonate what he or she is saying?" Look at yourself honestly, if you want to progress. If your Intuition answers "yes" and you want to sincerely make a change, focus on implementing the "opposite" quality into your life. You do this by pre-paving it into reality.

For example, perhaps someone has criticized you, saying that you never listen. Honestly ask yourself, "Is this true?" Your Intuition won't lie. If it is true, then set your intention to adopt the quality of being a good listener. Start by practicing the pre-paves in this book that will help you to focus on truly listening to others. Being a good listener is a rarity. If you can grab hold of this quality and make it your own, you will never be shy of friends.

We are each other's teachers. Be grateful to those who think enough of you to be honest with you. It takes courage. No one can offend you without your permission.

Pay no attention to what a critic says. A statue has never been erected in honor of a critic.

– Jean Sibelius

PRE-PAVE in Adversity

My mind is open to new ideas.

PRE-PAVE: *My mind is open to new ideas.*

S ome people become like psychological antiques, stuck in a certain way of thinking. In essence, an opportunity could come their way and they wouldn't even see it for lack of an open mind. When we pre-pave an open mind, we open ourselves to seeing things we would not otherwise see.

Through adversity, we can choose to be open to new ideas and concepts. It means looking outside of the box for solutions and listening to the ideas of others with the curiosity of a child.

There is no security on Earth. There is only opportunity.

– General Douglas MacArthur

PRE-PAVE in Adversity

Today I take a vacation from
my problems.

PRE-PAVE: *Today I take a vacation from my problems.*

Spend time today seeing the humor in life's experiences. Look at a situation you might currently be in that you would call a challenge. Choose to see the humor in it. Believe me, whatever you look for, you will find. Get right into the feeling of the humor and allow yourself to lighten up about your problems.

There is a classic line from the movie, *"What About Bob"* starring Richard Dreyfuss and Bill Murray. Dreyfuss plays a psychiatrist named Dr. Leo Marvin. Bill Murray plays Bob, a neurotic patient who won't leave Marvin alone, to the extent of following him on vacation. In his utter frustration, the doctor finally comes up with the answer to get Bob to leave him alone. He gives him a prescription: "Take a vacation from your problems."

Every now and then get away from your work, for when you return, your judgment will be surer.

When you take a vacation from your problems, you give your mind a break. When you return, you come back with a refreshed outlook and new solutions. Benjamin Franklin said it well, "Every now and then get away from your work, for when you return, your judgment will be surer."

Take a vacation from your problems. See the humor in life. When you smile and laugh, your vibration immediately changes. It brightens up and expands. You begin to vibrate goodness and draw to you new-found ways of coming up with solutions.

You cannot solve a problem with the same mind that created it.

– Wayne Dyer

PAVING IT FORWARD
in Faith

Although the search for the meaning of life is universal, spirituality is a very personal thing. I can honestly say that finding my spiritual path was the one true thing that changed my negative habits of thinking to the positive. My faith transformed my life from mediocre to phenomenal. Using the Law of Attraction to create what you want is only the first step. Finding the true meaning of life is the Ultimate. When you surrender your focus to a Higher Power, you take the Law of Attraction to a new level. By Higher Power, I am referring to what some call God, the Universe or the Source of all abundance. Whatever term I use below, I am referring to that great Power that created you and sustains you every moment.

This great Power created Universes upon Universes and is the owner of all abundance. When you align yourself with this Source of all, you become a magnet that attracts what this encompasses. Think about it; how vast this actually is. It is infinite, limitless, as is your ability to create.

To pre-pave in Spirit or Faith means that when you pre-pave, you bring that Higher Power into your thoughts. Watch the strength of your ability to create magnify exponentially. You do this by waking up in the morning and rather than just being grateful for what you have, acknowledge God as the Giver. Everything that you do and have, acknowledge where it has come from. In this way, you become awake to the Divine Power that is right within you.

As a young girl, I was very spiritual. I have my parents to thank for that. They provided me with a spiritual environment early on. It was a training I became especially grateful for later in life. I was raised in an environment of daily devotion, not just church on Sundays. The habit stuck with me as a teenager and, often, I would meet my mother at church over lunch when I was attending university. There were years throughout my childhood that I expressed the desire to become a nun. Again, in my thirties, my desire resurfaced. I decided for certain at this time, that it wasn't the life path for me. I had a keen desire to serve, but I discovered that it was my calling to serve on the outside and make a difference in other ways. I believe that is why I have been guided to write and teach.

On the flip side of the coin, I call my twenties my dark years. I was living thousands of miles from my home town. I had no choice but to discover myself. For ten years, I literally took a break from having any faith whatsoever. I remember going to church maybe a few times throughout those years, for a wedding or special occasion only. I don't recall spending any time at all in prayer or mindfulness. I guess unknowingly, I'd decided I had had enough; I would go it alone, or so I thought. Perhaps I was rebelling. I'm not even really sure of my motive, but I do know that I spent those years sorting through insecurities and a heap of challenges. In reality, I was miserable. It wasn't until a major relationship break-up at the age of thirty that I woke up and re-discovered the importance of Spirit in my life. It was then that I found the spiritual path that was to change my life forever.

I have since followed the teachings of Paramahansa Yogananda and have dedicated this book to the great spiritual Master who saved my life. After spending ten long years in oblivion to the true meaning of life, I now found myself asking the important questions: "What was it all for? How could I find true happiness? Did it even exist?" Everything in my life was changing, and continued to change daily as I absorbed the teachings like a thirsty sponge.

I discovered that God was not someone to pray to when you needed something. I learned that this world was just a dream and that a spark of the Divine was right within me. I learned that all along I had been seeking happiness in the things of the world, when it was to be found within me, within that Spark. Everything I had learned spiritually as a child now made much more sense to me. I could understand it from a higher level. Before, I had thought spirituality was something I should practice in order to be good or to be saved. I now realized that spirituality was the way to happiness, not something you did out of guilt. This new path made me discover true happiness, bubbling up from within; happiness that no one or nothing outside of me could take away.

I spent the next few years in a process of total metamorphosis. My whole belief system was awakened with a newfound understanding. I studied ancient Eastern philosophy, metaphysics and the healing arts. I learned about the power of thought and how it could change matter. The Universe provided for me the perfect environment upon which I could learn my most treasured lessons with this new knowledge. I received each challenge with enthusiasm. I knew what I was becoming through it and I embraced each experience with passion.

Two decades later, I continue to learn, but from an awakened awareness that I would not trade for anything of this world. Each day continues to be a stage for my own personal growth with its challenges and rewards. I experience just as many tests now as ever. But I see the Divine Hand behind everything and the true purpose of what life's challenges are trying to teach me. My greatest desire is to share this heightened awareness with others. I am passionate about helping people shift their consciousness to the positive. That is what I know to be my gift. I can teach people that with the right attitude, life is phenomenal. Attitude isn't the most important thing. It's the only thing.

With the next few pre-paves, I will show you how I have *Paved It Forward - In Faith* over the last several years. These are spiritual pre-paves that have transformed my life. If they resonate at all within you, perhaps they will shift your consciousness as they did mine.

PRE-PAVE in Faith

Today I focus on Love.

At the end of life, God doesn't care about what you accomplished. It matters not whether you found your Soul mate, landed your ultimate job, or bought your dream home on the bluff. He asks you this: *"Did you love Me?"* and *"Did you give My love to others?"* How is that for giving perspective on life? What a thought that is. How freeing is it to know that the purpose of life has nothing to do with externals. It all has to do with your state of mind. It is about how much you choose to love. That is something that is totally within your reach. It is your choice.

So, how to love the Divine? You need to have a concept of God that you can grab hold of and love. You need to have the passion that makes you race to your meditation seat to want to be with Him.

What if I asked you to love someone named Harry, and I told you he was a wonderful person. You could believe that, but you could not love him without meeting him and getting to know him first. So it is with God. You cannot love someone you don't know. In meditation, sitting in silence to feel God's presence, you get to know Him. And once you know Him, you cannot help but love Him.

> *Just as a candle cannot burn without fire,*
> *men cannot live without a spiritual life.*
>
> *– Buddha*

PRE-PAVE in Faith

Today I focus on God, for the
joy of it.

PRE-PAVE: *Today I focus on God, for the joy of it.*

As a child, I remember often I would focus on God out of fear. I wanted to be sure that when I died I would make it to a place called "heaven". When I sincerely look back on it, I didn't find it fun. More than not, it was a chore.

What I know now is that focusing on God **is** fun. We are on a ball whirling in space and there is a great Being who created and sustains it all. How thrilling is it to focus on this great Being! If Einstein walked through your door right now, would you not be interested in giving him your attention and asking him a few questions? Instead, our society races to the newsstand to see what the movie stars are eating for breakfast. What a shame. The Master of the Universe is beating within your heart, waiting for your attention. You could not move your arm if He did not give you the power to do so. He is closer than your heartbeat.

One of the greatest things my spiritual path taught me was to fall in Love. I fell in Love with wanting to be in Love with God. There is no substitute for this. If you can get this feeling and sustain it, life will never be the same for you. Trust me. You cannot go back to the other way of thinking. It is like the person who has had a near-death experience. They can never forget what they saw and felt. It is impossible. One glimpse, and they are changed forever.

If you could feel but a particle of Divine Love, so great would it be, you could not contain it.

– Paramahansa Yogananda

PRE-PAVE in Faith

I am non-attached to the
results.

PRE-PAVE: *I am non-attached to the results.*

Whatever you are creating, be non-attached to the results. It is a really free way to live. Watch the amazing results you reap through this attitude.

The material man plants a seed and cares for the plant daily with great attention. The plant is eaten by insects. He curses the insects for eating the plant that he worked so hard to grow. The spiritual man, on the other hand, plants a seed and cares for the plant with the same care and attention. The plant is eaten by insects. He plants another seed. He is non-attached. He does it for the joy he finds in the planting.

With this attitude of non-attachment, the spiritual man resonates success and, therefore, draws to him future success. The material man resonates frustration and disappointment which, of course, then draws to him more scenarios to be disappointed.

When you are attached to the outcome of a scenario, you put resistance around your desire. It creates an energy that pushes away that which you seek. Whatever you do, be non-attached to the outcome. Do your best and release the results.

> *The awakened sages call a person wise when all his undertakings are free from anxiety about results.*
>
> *– The Bhagavad Gita*

God and I are One.
(God has become me.)

PRE-PAVE: *God and I are One. (God has become me.)*

If you want to tune in with Spirit, this is an awesome pre-pave. This pre-pave is the quickest method of rising above the effects of past tendencies that you feel might be trying to find you. It can actually lessen the blow of results from past bad karma.

When you recognize yourself as One with the Creator, you cannot experience karma. You rise above it. God is above karma, so when you acknowledge that you are One with Him, then you are also above karma.

Another way to express this thought in words that ensure you are feeling it with the right attitude is this: "God has become me." In this way you know that you and God are One and yet He is still the Doer and the Creator. He is the ocean and you are the wave. The ocean can exist without the wave, but the wave cannot exist without the ocean.

PRE-PAVE in Faith

I am a child of God. God
loves me. Everything is fine.

PRE-PAVE: *I am a child of God. God loves me. Everything is fine.*

Lake Shrine is a serene and spiritual oasis situated in the heart of Pacific Palisades, California. I frequent it as often as possible, usually once a year. The Lake is surrounded by meditation gardens honoring churches of all religions, adorning statues of Buddha, Jesus, Krishna and other great Masters. At the top is a meditation temple.

A monk who serves at the Lake tells a story of a business-man who was healed one day in the gardens. This man had come to him for counseling. He was very perplexed with life, severely struggling both at work and home. He came to see the Brother for some guidance. After listening to him, Brother gave him the task of going down to the lake where the meditation gardens were. He suggested a walk around the lake chanting the above pre-pave, "I am a child of God. God loves me. Everything is fine".

He told the man to put his whole heart into it; to really feel it, excluding any other thought for one whole hour. When the hour was up, the man walked up the long outdoor staircase back to the temple. He found Brother and exclaimed, "I am healed!" Brother wasn't surprised. He knew the healing power of this affirmation.

I have used this so often in my life. Any time the world seems to want to cave in on me, and all else fails, I turn to this pre-pave. I hold onto it in my consciousness for dear life. I can honestly say that this pre-pave can heal anything. Practice it any time, especially when you need it the most.

PRE-PAVE in Faith

I acknowledge the true
Source of all abundance.

PRE-PAVE: *I acknowledge the true Source of all abundance.*

If you think it is your boss that signs your pay-cheque, or your spouse that provides you with love and support, think again. It is the Divine who is doing these things for you, through these people. God will provide all of your needs, when you trust that He is the true provider. This pre-pave is about trusting that your needs will always be met.

When you believe that external circumstances are responsible for your needs being met, you are limited to what these people can provide you in human form. When you know that the Universe is providing for you, there are no limits. This is why you don't need to ask the why or the how. Send your desires out and know that you will be provided for. It may be done for you through this person, or through that job, but it is the Source of all abundance that is ultimately providing it.

When you acknowledge the Divine as the Giver, there are no limits to what you can have, do or be.

Anything we turn in the direction of God is a prayer.
— St. Ignatius Loyola

PRE-PAVE in Faith

Work through my hands.
Think through my mind.
Love through my heart.

PRE-PAVE: *Work through my hands. Think through my mind. Love through my heart.*

This pre-pave invites God to use you as a channel. What amazing things you can accomplish when you acknowledge the Doer behind everything.

God uses willing instruments to fulfill our needs. He won't just manifest them, but will fulfill our needs through people willing to help. That is how the Universe manifests what we focus on. Today, focus on being the instrument that helps others create. When you are the channel, you open up the energy for so much to come to you. But that is not the reason you do it. Today, your focus is on being the assistant because it feels great to serve.

This pre-pave is most powerful by using it as an affirmation and chanting it inwardly throughout the day, many times. Keep it rolling in your mind as you go through your daily routine.

PRE-PAVE in Faith

Today I focus on listening.

PRE-PAVE: *Today I focus on listening.*

What if you had a friend and that friend came to visit you? What if he sat with you for an hour telling you all of the things he needed of you? What if he came back again the next day and did the same thing and each day repeated this similar experience? What kind of friendship would that be? This is how God feels when we come daily with our prayer requests. We sometimes even come asking why our yesterday's requests were not fulfilled.

Change your focus to that of a true friend. Sit in silence, prayer or meditation and listen. Cultivate a deep, unconditional relationship with the Divine.

When Mother Teresa was asked how she prays, she responded, "I listen."

PRE-PAVE in Faith

I seek happiness right within me.

PRE-PAVE: *I seek happiness right within me.*

Whether you acknowledge it or not on the conscious level, there is but one purpose of life. It is to be happy. Happiness is not found in the material things of this world. It is a consciousness that bubbles from within. When you sincerely walk the spiritual path, you find everything you seek.

Everyone is chasing the will-of-the-wisp they expect will give them happiness when all the while it has been, and always will be, right within themselves.

PRE-PAVE in Faith

For one whole day, I see
the good in everyone and
everything.

PRE-PAVE: *For one whole day, I see the good in everyone and everything.*

The great sages of India caution against three major deterrents to spiritual progress: criticism, complaining and gossip. Refrain from all three today. See the good in everyone. See the good in everything. And keep your own counsel.

What you think and talk about, you bring into your experience. To progress on the spiritual path, you must shift your energy to that of seeing the good in all.

PRE-PAVE in Faith

Today I focus on seeing God
in everything.

PRE-PAVE: *Today I focus on seeing God in everything.*

When you play the game of life, and you become attached to the drama, you will get hurt. Be non-attached to everything but God. See His face behind every flower, in every blade of grass. Hear His voice in the voices of children and your loved ones. Realize His hand behind everything that comes to you.

This pre-pave is especially helpful when dealing with difficult people. When you focus on this pre-pave, it will help you see people in a whole new light. You are given a greater understanding of the situation. Inevitably, it changes potential adversity into peace.

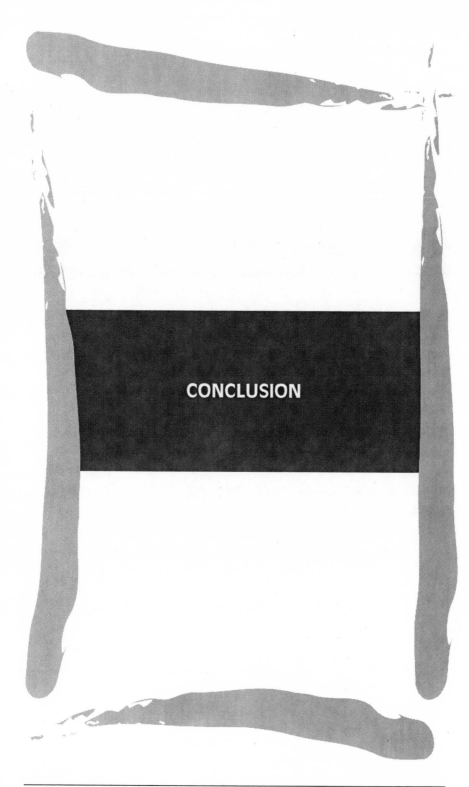

CONCLUSION

CONCLUSION

This is no ordinary book. It is a road map leading you to a way of life that can change your destiny. It is one thing to be inspired when reading an uplifting passage. It is quite another to embrace what you read and truly make it come alive in your life. By applying a mere handful of the pre-paves in this book, you will instantly realize the true power of *Paving It Forward*.

The pre-paves are summarized here for you in this chapter for easy reference. I challenge you to use those that resonate with you the most. Create your own that are unique to your lifestyle. Whatever you are inspired to create in this life will be easy to accomplish when you pave forward what you want with conviction. Embrace pre-paving as a life-long habit and watch your destiny change before your eyes. **You will see it when you believe it.**

I pre-pave every segment of my day. Life is precious! I want to feel great all of the time. No matter what goes on around me, pre-paving is my escape hatch. It pushes me toward focusing on what I want. The moment I send out a positive pre-pave, an inner silent happiness comes over me like a wave. I immediately start to feel at peace, like everything is going to be okay. I know that what I am paving forward, I am creating.

There is nothing more important in the Law of Attraction than feeling good. Your vibration is made up of your thoughts, feelings and intentions. You are continuously sending out a frequency into the Universe. You receive back according to what you are resonating or vibrating. Pre-paving instantly raises your vibration. It puts you into alignment to receive what you want.

Become aware of your thoughts during the day. The moment you find yourself in a state of worry, anxiety or fear, pave forward what you want instead. Turn your worries into positive pre-paves. In a moment of anger, redirect that pent-up energy into a passionate pre-pave instead. Anger is an awesome catalyst to pre-pave. Simply redirect the energy toward what you want. You can create an amazing life by doing this.

All day you are intending, and what you intend you create. Consciously intend your day by *Paving It Forward*, every step of the way.

SUMMARY

The Law of Attraction

Things of the same vibration or frequency are attracted to one another. Like attracts like.

The Law of Deliberate Creation

The recipe for consciously creating includes these ingredients:

1. Intuition: Being clear on what you want.
2. Desire: Unwavering focus on what you want.
3. Belief: Matching your beliefs with your desires.
4. Action: Making a move and paving it forward.

The Law of Allowing

I am that which I am, and I allow others to be as they are.

The Law of Giving

That which you give, you receive.

Paving it Forward – in the Morning

I feel great today.

Something wonderful is going to happen today.

Today I will deeply connect with people.

Today, I easily accomplish all I need to.

Today I make a fresh start.

I expect the best.

Today is a gift.

It's going to be a great day.

I love my life.

Paving it Forward – at Work

I arrive early for work and mentally prepare for the day.

I am valued for what I do.

I work with enthusiasm today.

I am passionate about what I do.

I focus on solutions today.

I focus on serving others.

My meetings are successful beyond my expectations.

I will shake up the world if I have to!

I sincerely listen to my customer.

I react with kindness and professionalism to all that happens.

I treat this company as if it were my own.

This is not a job; it is a way of life.

I follow my dreams.

It feels good to admit my mistakes and move toward a solution.

I see and expect the best in others.

I reward myself.

Today I will make someone's day!

Paving it Forward – in Family

My children are safe.

Today I am aware of the non-verbal communication from my children.

My family loves and accepts me just as I am.

I deeply connect with my family.

I honor my mother and father.

Paving it Forward – in Food

Bless this food.

I choose foods today that promote a calm state of mind.

I eat when I'm hungry and I stop when I'm full.

Every day I feel thinner and thinner.

Today I eat my meals in silence.

Paving it Forward – at Night

I pre-pave a restful sleep.

Tonight I will fall asleep quickly and sleep right through the night.

I receive important messages in my dreams.

I dream dreams of beauty and happy experiences.

I am conscious in my dreams.

I honestly and sincerely review the day.

I pray for others.

I am grateful for _____.

Paving it Forward – in Love

I treat myself with respect, patience and understanding.

Today I heal one relationship in my life.

We greet each other with respect.

Today I release the past.

I release relationships that no longer serve me.

I show my true self to others.

I am special. I appreciate my own uniqueness.

I see myself honestly.

Today I see the best in others.

Today I focus on Understanding others.

Whatever I want out of a relationship, I focus on giving it.

I am that which I am, and I allow others to be as they are.

Today I keep my vibration high and uplift others around me.

I approach all others today with Compassion.

Paving it Forward – in Creating

Today I spend some time in Silence.

I follow my Intuition.

I ask myself today, "How do I feel?" "What do I want?"

I cultivate desires that are in tune with my higher purpose.

Today I spend time writing about what I want.

I spend time today dreaming big.

I focus on my goals.

I will persevere.

I know I can do this.

I expect the best and I believe in the best.

I associate with people who support my goals.

I follow through on my resolutions.

Paving it Forward – in Giving

Whatever I need, I focus on giving it.

I give for the joy of giving.

I give my greatest gift, myself.

Paving it Forward – in Travel

I pre-pave safety. I am safe.

My car is reliable. I can always depend on it.

I reach my destination quickly and efficiently.

I choose the perfect place for my trip.

I'm going to have a great time.

Paving it Forward – in Health

I pre-pave good health.

I think, speak and act of health.

I replace my bodily cells daily with new healthy cells.

I fill my body with Light.

I pray for the healing of others.

Paving it Forward – in Wealth

I appreciate my house, my electricity, my telephone, my car.

All of my needs are met, now and always.

I need $_____ to do or to buy _____.

Every day I feel more and more wealthy.

I keep focused on my financial success.

Paving it Forward – in Adversity

Change no circumstance in my life. Change me.

Today I change one thing about myself.

My environment is perfect for me.

This world is a dream.

I am compassionate with myself and others.

I face my tests with courage.

I am becoming the person I want to be.

Today I will do something I have never done before.

I release one thing today that no longer serves me.

I simplify my life.

I react to every situation today with calmness.

I am calm, I am peaceful.

Today it is easy to be patient with all people and all circumstances.

I allow things to be less than perfect today.

Today I choose to be happy.

Today I clean up one area of my life.

Today I either release the opinions of others or I learn from them.

My mind is open to new ideas.

Today I take a vacation from my problems.

Paving it Forward – in Faith

Today I focus on Love.

Today I focus on God, for the joy of it.

I am non-attached to the results.

God and I are One. (God has become me.)

I am a child of God. God loves me. Everything is fine.

I acknowledge the true Source of all abundance.

Work through my hands. Think through my mind.
Love through my heart.

Today I focus on listening.

I seek happiness right within me.

For one whole day, I see the good in everyone and everything.

Today I focus on seeing God in everything.

The Elisabeth Fayt Collection

Pre-Pave Your Day

Companion Card Deck to "Paving it Forward"

This beautiful card deck features 60 cards to pre-pave your day. There are three categories of pre-paves in this deck: Work, Love and Life. Choose a card in the category you desire, or choose randomly from the entire deck. Pull one card or as many as you like. Whatever card you choose, pre-pave it with conviction, followed by a feeling of gratitude that it is already accomplished.

This deck helps you make pre-paving a habit, lining up the energy for success. It makes an excellent gift to introduce loved ones to the power of pre-paving.

The Universal Law of Abundance - *Two Disc Set*

Learning to Give and Receive

We live in an abundant Universe. Everything we want and need is readily available to us, when we learn how to Give & Receive in the right spirit.

Elisabeth Fayt will guide you through a journey of awareness to discover your own road map to Abundance. You will learn how to create at will, what you need; materially, emotionally and spiritually through the intricate law of Giving & Receiving for Abundance.

Transformation CD

The Energy of Change

A guided journey of abundance, healing and self-discovery using the powerful technique of pre-paving as shared in Elisabeth's book, "Paving it Forward".

This CD leads you through a series of mental exercises designed to assist you as you make change in your life. Selections include:

- Conscious Intention
- Gratitude
- Changing Habits
- Love
- Rain Shower Meditation

Elisabeth Fayt as heard on "Christina at Night"

Inspirational Gems & Stories

Listen in as Elisabeth shares the wisdom of ages with callers and introduces the transformational power of pre-paving, as explored in her book "Paving it Forward". Be inspired with short stories and other tidbits of wisdom. Perfect for listening in the car. Makes a great pass-along tool to share with friends and family.
Topics explored are:

- Focus
- Self Esteem
- Pre-Paving
- Hope & Faith
- The Power of Thought
- Relationships
- Service
- Happiness

**For more information on products, workshops & retreats
please visit www.pavingitforward.com**

BUY A SHARE OF THE FUTURE IN YOUR COMMUNITY

These certificates make great holiday, graduation and birthday gifts that can be personalized with the recipient's name. The cost of one S.H.A.R.E. or one square foot is $54.17. The personalized certificate is suitable for framing and will state the number of shares purchased and the amount of each share, as well as the recipient's name. The home that you participate in "building" will last for many years and will continue to grow in value.

Here is a sample SHARE certificate:

YES, I WOULD LIKE TO HELP!

I support the work that Habitat for Humanity does and I want to be part of the excitement! As a donor, I will receive periodic updates on your construction activities but, more importantly, I know my gift will help a family in our community realize the dream of homeownership. **I would like to SHARE in your efforts against substandard housing in my community!** *(Please print below)*

PLEASE SEND ME _____ SHARES at $54.17 EACH = $ $_____

In Honor Of: _____

Occasion: (Circle One)   HOLIDAY   BIRTHDAY   ANNIVERSARY

OTHER: _____

Address of Recipient: _____

Gift From: _____ *Donor Address:* _____

Donor Email: _____

I AM ENCLOSING A CHECK FOR $ $_____ PAYABLE TO HABITAT FOR HUMANITY <u>OR</u> PLEASE CHARGE MY VISA OR MASTERCARD *(CIRCLE ONE)*

Card Number _____ Expiration Date: _____

Name as it appears on Credit Card _____ Charge Amount $ _____

Signature _____

Billing Address _____

Telephone # Day _____ Eve _____

PLEASE NOTE: Your contribution is tax-deductible to the fullest extent allowed by law.
Habitat for Humanity • P.O. Box 1443 • Newport News, VA 23601 • 757-596-5553
www.HelpHabitatforHumanity.org

LaVergne, TN USA
27 August 2009
156113LV00002B/85/P